Barbara Jo Brothers
Editor

Couples
and Body Therapy

Couples and Body Therapy has been co-published simultaneously as *Journal of Couples Therapy,* Volume 10, Number 2 2001.

Pre-publication
REVIEWS,
COMMENTARIES,
EVALUATIONS . . .

"*Couples and Body Therapy* is a wonderful revisiting and blending of two significant fields of knowledge and practice. Once digested, one wonders how the therapist can focus on the couple without addressing the bodies they inhabit."

Cindy Ashkins, PhD, LCSW, LMT
Couples Psychotherapist
and Licensed Bodyworker in Private Practice,
Metairie, NC

Couples and Body Therapy

Couples and Body Therapy has been co-published simultaneously as *Journal of Couples Therapy*, Volume 10, Number 2 2001.

The *Journal of Couples Therapy* Monographic "Separates"

Below is a list of "separates," which in serials librarianship means a special issue simultaneously published as a special journal issue or double-issue and as a "separate" hardbound monograph. (This is a format which we also call a "DocuSerial.")

"Separates" are published because specialized libraries or professionals may wish to purchase a specific thematic issue by itself in a format which can be separately cataloged and shelved, as opposed to purchasing the journal on an on-going basis. Faculty members may also more easily consider a "separate" for classroom adoption.

"Separates" are carefully classified separately with the major book jobbers so that the journal tie-in can be noted on new book order slips to avoid duplicate purchasing.

You may wish to visit Haworth's website at . . .

http://www.HaworthPress.com

. . . to search our online catalog for complete tables of contents of these separates and related publications.

You may also call 1-800-HAWORTH (outside US/Canada: 607-722-5857), or Fax 1-800-895-0582 (outside US/Canada: 607-771-0012), or e-mail at:

getinfo@haworthpressinc.com

Couples and Body Therapy, edited by Barbara Jo Brothers, MSW, BCD, CGP (Vol. 10, No. 2, 2001). *"A wonderful revisiting and blending of two significant fields. Once digested, one wonders how the therapist can focus on the couple without addressing the bodies they inhabit." (Cindy Ashkins, PhD, LCSW, LMT, Couples Psychotherapist and Licensed Bodyworker in Private Practice, Metairie, North Carolina)*

The Personhood of the Therapist, edited by Barbara Jo Brothers, MSW, BCSW (Vol. 9, No. 3/4, 2000). *Through suggestions, techniques, examples, and case studies, this book will help you develop a great sense of openness about yourself and your feelings, enabling you to offer clients more effective services.*

Couples Connecting: Prerequisites of Intimacy, edited by Barbara Jo Brothers, MSW, BCSW (Vol. 9, No. 1/2, 2000). *"Brothers views marriage as an ideal context for the psychological and spiritual evolution of human beings, and invites therapists to reflect on the role they can play in facilitating this. Readers are sure to recognize their clients among the examples given and to return to their work with a renewed vision of the possibilities for growth and change." (Eleanor D. Macklin, PhD, Emeritus Professor and former Director of the Marriage and Family Therapy program, Syracuse University, New York)*

Couples Therapy in Managed Care: Facing the Crisis, edited by Barbara Jo Brothers, MSW, BCSW (Vol. 8, No. 3/4, 1999). *Provides social workers, psychologists, and counselors with an overview of the negative effects of the managed care industry on the quality of mental health care. Within this book, you will discover the paradoxes that occur with the mixing of business principles and service principles and find valuable suggestions on how you can creatively cope within the managed care context. With* Couples Therapy in Managed Care, *you will learn how you can remain true to your own integrity and still get paid for your work and offer quality services within the current context of managed care.*

Couples and Pregnancy: Welcome, Unwelcome, and In-Between, edited by Barbara Jo Brothers, MSW, BCSW (Vol. 8, No. 2, 1999). *Gain valuable insight into how pregnancy and birth have a profound psychological effect on the parents' relationship, especially on their experience of intimacy.*

Couples, Trauma, and Catastrophes, edited by Barbara Jo Brothers, MSW, BCSW (Vol. 7, No. 4, 1998). *Helps therapists and counselors working with couples facing major crises and trauma.*

Couples: A Medley of Models, edited by Barbara Jo Brothers, MSW, BCSW, BCD (Vol. 7, No. 2/3, 1998). *"A wonderful set of authors who illuminate different corners of relationships. This book belongs on your shelf . . . but only after you've read it and loved it."* (Derek Paar, PhD, Associate Professor of Psychology, Springfield College, Massachusetts)

When One Partner Is Willing and the Other Is Not, edited by Barbara Jo Brothers, MSW, BCSW (Vol. 7, No. 1, 1997). *"An engaging variety of insightful perspectives on resistance in couples therapy."* (Stan Taubman, DSW, Director of Managed Care, Alameda County Behavioral Health Care Service, Berkeley, California; Author, Ending the Struggle Against Yourself)

Couples and the Tao of Congruence, edited by Barbara Jo Brothers, MSW, BCSW (Vol. 6, No. 3/4, 1996). *"A library of information linking Virginia Satir's teaching and practice of creative improvement in human relations and the Tao of Congruence. . . . A stimulating reader."* (Josephine A. Bates, DSW, BD, retired mental health researcher and family counselor, Lake Preston, South Dakota)

Couples and Change, edited by Barbara Jo Brothers, MSW, BCSW (Vol. 6, No. 1/2, 1996). *This enlightening book presents readers with Satir's observations–observations that show the difference between thinking with systems in mind and thinking linearly–of process, interrelatedness, and attitudes.*

Couples: Building Bridges, edited by Barbara Jo Brothers, MSW, BCSW (Vol. 5, No. 4, 1996). *"This work should be included in the library of anyone considering to be a therapist or who is one or who is fascinated by the terminology and conceptualizations which the study of marriage utilizes."* (Irv Loev, PhD, MSW-ACP, LPC, LMFT, private practitioner)

Couples and Countertransference, edited by Barbara Jo Brothers, MSW, BCSW (Vol. 5, No. 3, 1995). *"I would recommend this book to beginning and advanced couple therapists as well as to social workers and psychologists. . . . This book is a wealth of information."* (International Transactional Analysis Association)

Power and Partnering, edited by Barbara Jo Brothers, MSW, BCSW (Vol. 5, No. 1/2, 1995). *"Appeals to therapists and lay people who find themselves drawn to the works of Virginia Satir and Carl Jung. Includes stories and research data satisfying the tastes of both left- and right-brained readers."* (Virginia O. Felder, ThM, Licensed Marriage and Family Therapist, private practice, Atlanta, Georgia)

Surpassing Threats and Rewards: Newer Plateaus for Couples and Coupling, edited by Barbara Jo Brothers, MSW, BCSW (Vol. 4, No. 3/4, 1995). *Explores the dynamics of discord, rejection, and blame in the coupling process and provides practical information to help readers understand marital dissatisfaction and how this dissatisfaction manifests itself in relationships.*

Attraction and Attachment: Understanding Styles of Relationships, edited by Barbara Jo Brothers, MSW, BCSW (Vol. 4, No. 1/2, 1994). *"Ideas on working effectively with couples. . . . I strongly recommend this book for those who want to have a better understanding of the complex dynamics of couples and couples therapy."* (Gilbert J. Greene, PhD, ACSW, Associate Professor, College of Social Work, The Ohio State University)

Peace, War, and Mental Health: Couples Therapists Look at the Dynamics, edited by Barbara Jo Brothers, MSW, BCSW (Vol. 3, No. 4, 1993). *Discover how issues of world war and peace relate to the dynamics of couples therapy in this thought-provoking book.*

Couples Therapy, Multiple Perspectives: In Search of Universal Threads, edited by Barbara Jo Brothers, MSW, BCSW (Vol. 3, No. 2/3, 1993). *"A very sizeable team of couples therapists has scoured the countryside in search of the most effective methods for helping couples improve their relationships. . . . The bibliographies are a treasury of worthwhile references."* (John F. Sullivan, EdS, Marriage and Family Counselor in Private Practice, Newburgh, New York)

Spirituality and Couples: Heart and Soul in the Therapy Process, edited by Barbara Jo Brothers, MSW, BCSW (Vol. 3, No. 1, 1993). *"Provides an array of reflections particularly for therapists beginning to address spirituality in the therapeutic process."* (Journal of Family Psychotherapy)

Equal Partnering: A Feminine Perspective, edited by Barbara Jo Brothers, MSW, BCSW (Vol. 2, No. 4, 1992). *Designed to help couples, married or not, understand how to achieve a balanced, equal partnership.*

Coupling . . . What Makes Permanence? edited by Barbara Jo Brothers, MSW, BCSW (Vol. 2, No. 3, 1991). *"Explores what it is that makes for a relationship in which each partner can grow and develop while remaining attached to another." (The British Journal of Psychiatry)*

Virginia Satir: Foundational Ideas, edited by Barbara Jo Brothers, MSW, BCSW (Vol. 2, No. 1/2, 1991). *"The most thorough conglomeration of her ideas available today. Done in the intimate, yet clear fashion you would expect from Satir herself. . . . Well worth getting your hands damp to pick up this unique collection." (Journal of Family Psychotherapy)*

Intimate Autonomy: Autonomous Intimacy, edited by Barbara Jo Brothers, MSW, BCSW (Vol. 1, No. 3/4, 1991). *"A fine collection of chapters on one of the most difficult of human tasks–getting close enough to another to share the warmth and benefits of that closeness without losing what is precious in our separations." (Howard Halpern, PhD, Author,* How to Break Your Addiction to a Person*)*

Couples on Coupling, edited by Barbara Jo Brothers, MSW, BCSW (Vol. 1, No. 2, 1990). *"A variety of lenses through which to view relationships, each providing a different angle for seeing patterns, strengths, and problems and for gaining insight into a given couple system." (Suzanne Imes, PhD, Clinical Psychologist, Private Practice, Atlanta, Georgia; Adjunct Assistant Professor of Psychology, Georgia State University)*

Couples
and Body Therapy

Barbara Jo Brothers
Editor

Couples and Body Therapy has been co-published simultaneously as *Journal of Couples Therapy*, Volume 10, Number 2 2001.

The Haworth Press, Inc.
New York • London • Oxford

Couples and Body Therapy has been co-published simultaneously as *Journal of Couples Therapy* ™, Volume 10, Number 2 2001.

The development, preparation, and publication of this work has been undertaken with great care. However, the publisher, employees, editors, and agents of The Haworth Press and all imprints of The Haworth Press, Inc., including The Haworth Medical Press® and Pharmaceutical Products Press®, are not responsible for any errors contained herein or for consequences that may ensue from use of materials or information contained in this work. Opinions expressed by the author(s) are not necessarily those of The Haworth Press, Inc.

The Haworth Press, Inc., 10 Alice Street, Binghamton, NY 13904-1580 USA

Cover design by Thomas J. Mayshock Jr.

Library of Congress Cataloging-in-Publication Data

Couples and body therapy / Barbara Jo Brothers, editor.
     p. cm.
    "Co-published simultaneously as Journal of couples therapy, vol. 10, no. 2, 2001."
    Includes bibliographical references and index.
    ISBN 0-7890-1654-0 (alk. paper)–ISBN 0-7890-1655-9 (alk. paper)
    1. Marital psychotherapy. 2. Mind and body therapies. I. Brothers, Barbara Jo, 1940–
II. Journal of couples therapy III. Title.

RC488.5 .C6425 2001
616.89′156–dc21
                                               2001039151

Indexing, Abstracting & Website/Internet Coverage

This section provides you with a list of major indexing & abstracting services. That is to say, each service began covering this periodical during the year noted in the right column. Most Websites which are listed below have indicated that they will either post, disseminate, compile, archive, cite or alert their own Website users with research-based content from this work. (This list is as current as the copyright date of this publication.)

Abstracting, Website/Indexing Coverage .... Year When Coverage Began

- *BUBL Information Service: An Internet-based Information Service for the UK Higher Education Community <bubl.ac.uk/>* . 1995

- *CNPIEC Reference Guide: Chinese National Directory of Foreign Periodicals* 1995

- *e-psyche, LLC <www.e-psyche.net>* 2001

- *Family Studies Database (online and CD/ROM) <www.nisc.com>* .. 1995

- *Family Violence & Sexual Assault Bulletin* 1991

- *FINDEX <www.publist.com>* 1999

- *Referativnyi Zhurnal (Abstracts Journal of the All-Russian Institute of Scientific and Technical Information–in Russian)* 1991

- *Social Services Abstracts <www.csa.com>* 1991

- *Social Work Abstracts* 1991

- *Sociological Abstracts (SA) <www.csa.com>* 1991

- *Studies on Women Abstracts* 1991

- *Violence and Abuse Abstracts: A Review of Current Literature on Interpersonal Violence (VAA)* 1994

Special Bibliographic Notes related to special journal issues
(separates) and indexing/abstracting:

- indexing/abstracting services in this list will also cover material in any "separate" that is co-published simultaneously with Haworth's special thematic journal issue or DocuSerial. Indexing/abstracting usually covers material at the article/chapter level.
- monographic co-editions are intended for either non-subscribers or libraries which intend to purchase a second copy for their circulating collections.
- monographic co-editions are reported to all jobbers/wholesalers/approval plans. The source journal is listed as the "series" to assist the prevention of duplicate purchasing in the same manner utilized for books-in-series.
- to facilitate user/access services all indexing/abstracting services are encouraged to utilize the co-indexing entry note indicated at the bottom of the first page of each article/chapter/contribution.
- this is intended to assist a library user of any reference tool (whether print, electronic, online, or CD-ROM) to locate the monographic version if the library has purchased this version but not a subscription to the source journal.
- individual articles/chapters in any Haworth publication are also available through the Haworth Document Delivery Service (HDDS).

Couples and Body Therapy

CONTENTS

ABOUT THE EDITOR

Barbara Jo Brothers, MSW, BCD, a Diplomate in Clinical Social Work, National Association of Social Workers, is in private practice in New Orleans. She received her BA from the University of Texas and her MSW from Tulane University, where she is currently on the faculty. She was Editor of *The Newsletter of the American Academy of Psychotherapists* from 1976 to 1985, and was Associate Editor of *Voices: The Art and Science of Psychotherapy* from 1979 to 1989. She has 30 years of experience, in both the public and private sectors, helping people to form skills that will enable them to connect emotionally. The author of numerous articles and book chapters on authenticity in human relating, she has advocated healthy, congruent communication that builds intimacy as opposed to destructive, incongruent communication which blocks intimacy. In addition to her many years of direct work with couples and families, Ms. Brothers has led numerous workshops on teaching communication in families and has also played an integral role in the development of training programs in family therapy for mental health workers throughout the Louisiana state mental health system. She is a board member of the Institute for International Connections, a non-profit organization for cross-cultural professional development focused on training and cross-cultural exchange with psychotherapists in Russia, in republics once part of what used to be the Soviet Union, and other Eastern European countries.

Preface

Mary Giuffra, Director of Research at the Institute for Core Energetics, mid-wifed much of this volume. Concerned about components too often ignored in psychotherapy–spirituality and the body–Giuffra set about finding, among a wide range of experts, many of the authors in this collection.

Giuffra's many years of experience in a variety of modes of psychotherapy have made her aware of the critical importance of involving the whole person in the therapy process. Body and spirit and mind are all one package. It is the task of the therapist to be part of a process of the restoration of essential harmony among the various facets of a given human being. Such integration is prerequisite to a constructive relationship between a couple. Mary Giuffra feels a responsibility to the mental health community, and to their patients, to raise consciousness about these facts.

Her own article traces her evolution from obstetric and pediatric nurse to Core Energetics therapist. She makes clear the basis and evidence for her belief in the importance of Core Energetics modality. We are indebted to her for sharing the fruits of her rich journey with us.

I am very grateful to Mary Giuffra for all the energy she used in helping to create *Couples and Body Therapy*.

Barbara Jo Brothers, Editor

[Haworth co-indexing entry note]: "Preface." Brothers, Barbara Jo. Co-published simultaneously in *Journal of Couples Therapy* (The Haworth Press, Inc.) Vol. 10, No. 2, 2001, p. xvii; and: *Couples and Body Therapy* (ed: Barbara Jo Brothers) The Haworth Press, Inc., 2001, p. xiii. Single or multiple copies of this article are available for a fee from The Haworth Document Delivery Service [1-800-342-9678, 9:00 a.m. - 5:00 p.m. (EST). E-mail address: getinfo@haworthpressinc.com].

Virginia Satir and Body-Mind-Soul

Barbara Jo Brothers

SUMMARY. Featured are excerpts from several edited, transcribed lectures, from 1972-1987, by Virginia Satir on the relationship between body, mind, and soul. The excerpts are woven together with comments, explications, and clarification by the author. *[Article copies available for a fee from The Haworth Document Delivery Service: 1-800-342-9678. E-mail address: <getinfo@haworthpressinc.com> Website: <http://www.HaworthPress.com> © 2001 by The Haworth Press, Inc. All rights reserved.]*

KEYWORDS. Body, mind, soul, affective, cognitive, verbal, non-verbal, cancer, congruence, double messages, interaction

Virginia Satir was about wholeness. Never one dimensional, she always included the body "in the equation" when training, treating, or educating human beings. Virginia considered the specific body-mind-soul of a given person to be one entity. A person is a "manifestation of Life" (Satir, 1987, tape 5) and, by definition, a sacred embodiment. She observed that matters of the spirit also have a direct relationship to styles of interaction. In her work with people, she would aim to stay tuned, at all times, to the three-in-one in herself as well as in the clients and trainees.

CONNECTING BODY AND SOUL

Universal Personal Resources

Making the connection between spirituality and sensuality–joining body and soul, if you will–Virginia (1983)[1] addresses what constitutes "self." The

---

[Haworth co-indexing entry note]: "Virginia Satir and Body-Mind-Soul." Brothers, Barbara Jo. Co-published simultaneously in *Journal of Couples Therapy* (The Haworth Press, Inc.) Vol. 10, No. 2, 2001, pp. 1-15; and: *Couples and Body Therapy* (ed: Barbara Jo Brothers) The Haworth Press, Inc., 2001, pp. 1-16. Single or multiple copies of this article are available for a fee from The Haworth Document Delivery Service [1-800-342-9678, 9:00 a.m. - 5:00 p.m. (EST). E-mail address: getinfo@haworthpressinc.com].

1

following excerpt comes after discussion of the role of the senses, under the heading "Universal Personal Resources." She is drawing a "Self Mandala" on the blackboard. She says:

> Now in the center I want you to make a circle and in that center I want you to write "I." This is all personal, there isn't anything else that isn't personal. Have you ever been aware that there is nothing impersonal in life? Everything is personal; it has to be. So let us forget that nonsense about being personal or impersonal; there isn't any such thing. If I'm doing it, I'm doing it; that's me and that's personal.
>   That is "I." And I want to write the word on the top: "sacred." And on the bottom I want to write: "holy"–and on one side I want to write: "cosmic joke" and on the other side: "cosmic event." (Banmen and Satir, 1983, pp. 241-242)

She goes on about the body, saying:

> Now every "I" . . . sits in a temple. And that temple, a place for the "I" to live, is a body. You can call it anything you want but I call [it] the temple–the body. It houses that "I," that sacred, holy, cosmic event and joke, which you are and I am–different things at different times. So everything physical would be in that, all the things we talk about as physical. . . . (Banmen and Satir, 1983, p. 242)

She goes on to say:

> The holes that we have we call the senses, but I would like you to see or hear, "Sense" and think, "Hole"–and when you think "hole," you think something moving back and forth. Something moving out, some-thing moving in. And without these holes we cannot live. We cannot live. . . . Each of those holes is capable of putting something out and taking something in. [They are] the literal channels for taking in and giving out. (1983, p. 244)

CONNECTING MIND AND HEART

Connecting mind and heart, Virginia explains the distinction between the cognitive message and the affective message:

> The cognitive comes from a totally different place than the affective. The cognitive is that which is made up of the "shoulds," the "oughts"

and intellectual output. . . . The affective is the body thermometer . . . it is the active manifestation of what is going on in the body. (1987, tape 5)

Profound problems are often created when a given Sam or Sally Jones' cognitive message doesn't match his/her affective message–when a person is feeling one thing and saying another.

> . . . it is possible for these two messages to be split. Cognitive goes this way and the affective goes that way. When we have that, we have what is called an "incongruent message," meaning that the words and the rest don't match. (1987, tape 5)

Virginia spoke of the power of inhuman system rules, dysfunctional rules taught by parents to children. She set up an exercise to demonstrate the potentially destructive effect of "I must never lie" as a cognitive message:

> "I can never lie." What did your body feel like [during this demonstration]?
> "Nonsense."
> Okay, but what is a nonsense feeling?
> "It's not true."
> It is an untruth and *our bodies love truth.* (Satir, 1987, tape 5)

Using the participants' sensual reaction to the demonstration, Virginia has pointed out the way body reacts to thought and feeling:

> How people convey things back and forth: the [definition] I give communication. I think that is a relatively easy definition: communication is the giving and receiving of information between two people. That's how it always goes. It is just giving and receiving information. When somebody coughs, what kind of information does the other one receive? Just ask yourself that. If you go beyond words and think about it, when you cross your legs, or you uncross your legs, or lift your head, or say "poof," or your skin color changes, or you get a lump some place, no matter what, all of that is communication. The giving and receiving of information. (1987, tape 5)

Virginia makes the point that physical symptoms are a message from the bodied aspect of the self.

These are her observations about the influence of thought and feeling on body and vice versa.

> I watched people, thousands of them. I have told you that I'm fifty-one years in the field this year, so you can imagine how many different

interactions I have seen over time. Lots and lots and lots of them. At a certain point . . . one day a grid appeared to me . . . I saw that the communication that was related to dysfunctional behavior was related to people not enjoying their lives and was one of these four forms. (1987, tape 5)[2]

Particularly in the beginning years of Virginia's professional career, circa 1948, therapy focused on the cognitive almost exclusively. Gestalt therapy was born later. Psychodrama was born even later. She goes on to say:

In information, there is (1) cognitive information, there is (2) emotional information, and there is (3) sensual information. What Ernie [Rossi] talks about in his book [on the psychobiology of healing] is that when the information from the endocrine system, the neurological system and the immune system don't find coding ways to connect with each other, they have to separate. *In the Western world we have given most of our attention to cognitive information.* We read it in a book, we see the words, and the words make the images, but reading it in a book doesn't show how the person is feeling or thinking or how they are gesturing or how they are breathing . . . so it is a totally different thing when we put it into a human context.

I want to give you just enough so that we get a good context for this. If you will remember, when I use information, it is on *all* levels . . . It is not about just giving words. (Satir, 1987, tape 5)

Most of our culture is not tuned in on the psychological level to that *emotional* information Virginia is talking about. And that is the vital difference. Blocking awareness of emotional information blocks awareness of our nature as whole beings. It also prepares the way for atrocities such as terrorist bombings and the tragedy at Waco at the Branch Davidian compound. All parties involved were focused on their respective causes, regardless of cost to the literal human beings involved.

Blocking that emotional information is a major obstacle to serious movement toward peace on any level–individual, family, or world. If I don't care how I feel or how you feel, I can do *any* sort of thing for a principle. That is where the inhumanity comes in–devotion to the cause above the effect on the human beings. Blocking or minimizing that emotional information is what people do when they take the super-reasonable stance[3] in communication. The person is, at such a point, trying to cope with the stress of feeling unworthy by simply *blocking* feeling: you can't feel bad about yourself if you are not feeling at all.

As I have said in other places (Brothers, 1987, 1989, pace Virginia Satir), a body also pays a high price for muting such information. It trains the glands to not perform their normal function simply by continually restraining their output–in Virginia's more colorful words, there being "a juice for every emotion." If the emotions don't flow, the "juices" don't flow.

Good therapists know the cognitive must not be emphasized at the expense of the affective. Virginia makes the connection between affect and the body:

> To finish this, I'm going to put it into an interactional frame. Here is the cognitive and the affective. That brings out the message, Then, somebody over here is receiving that message. Bear in mind that when somebody's cognitive message and affective message aren't together, they are coming from two different places. The cognitive comes from a totally different place than the affective. The cognitive is that which is made up of the "shoulds," the "oughts" and intellectual output, so to speak. The brain is very capable of doing all kinds of wonderful things all by itself. *The affective is the body thermometer. Remember that the body is the thermometer and it is the active manifestation of what is going on in the body* [body/mind/soul system].
> . . . Cognitive, in a way, is a "should" message and you can say that the affective is the "end" message. When I do the pull out here, I put the affective message on one side and the cognitive on the other. [Then] you can say that it is thought and feeling that don't go together. (Satir, 1987, tape 5)

Virginia's point is that, whatever a person says with words–whatever lie they tell either to self or to others–the truth in regard to affect *will* show in the body. I can "do cognitive" however I want to, but there is always the flow of the affective underneath the verbiage. However metaphorical the "dials and gauges," the body measures and displays feelings. If one is conscious in regard to one's interior processes, the feelings can be verbalized–and one can cry or sweat or blush. If the feelings are not conscious, not in awareness, the body still registers them–still quivers, gurgles, and crackles the chemistry and the electromagnetism. The therapist who has trained herself to watch the body of herself and of the other can see bodily manifestations and help bring them to the awareness of the other.

To spare clients the disrespect of "interpretation," Virginia was meticulously careful to only *describe* what she saw, then *maybe* inquire as to its meaning: "I see your eyebrows knit together right now. Are you aware of that?" Often all that was necessary was for her to just notice the body behavior and draw it to the person's attention. Usually, the person would then become aware of feeling angry or feeling puzzled–or whatever feeling went with the eyebrows.

Talking about cognition and affect was preliminary to Virginia's making her explanation of the need for one of her major vehicles[4]–Family Reconstruction.

> This [parent-child interaction] is where, I think, we learned about feeling. Affect is about feeling. Cognition is about the intellect. The mother, who cannot herself stand the idea that she is feeling afraid or that she is feeling guilty, whatever it is [that she is feeling], has to say to the child, "It isn't true what you see." Everyone of us . . . with very few exceptions, got this experience from our parents. The reason for it was not because they wanted to hurt us, but because the cognitive part of what they "should be" didn't match the way they felt. Then, the child tries to make sense out of this.
>
> This is where we come into the [family] reconstruction business. You can [then] understand how come you got such crazy messages. You couldn't find out what was going on. It was because the "should" of a person in your parent wasn't equal in their mind or [wasn't] available [so] that they could openly say where they were. They couldn't say they were afraid. They couldn't say they felt hurt or whatever it was. They had to do the defensive reaction.
>
> When you can get no validation cognitively or affectively, two people cannot communicate this way. It's confusing, and the kid in us doesn't comprehend and that's where schizophrenia shows itself. I learned that a long time ago. (Satir, 1987, tape 5)

CONGRUENCE AND COCKROACHES

In *Supernature,* biologist Lyall Watson describes an extremely interesting physical example.

Were the implications less profound, this would be almost funny; Janet Harker's experiment with a pair of *cockroaches* illustrates Virginia Satir's profound observation concerning the effects of the communication process on human beings. Well, Virginia had a good sense of humor:

> [Harker] . . . kept one group of cockroaches on a normal schedule and put a second group on a reverse timetable, with lights burning all night and darkness during the day. The second lot soon adapted to this situation and became active during the artificial night, so their rhythms were always out of phase with the control group. A subesophageal ganglion could easily be transplanted from a member of one group to a headless individual in the other, and it would impose its own rhythm on the recipient; but if the second cockroach kept its own pacemaker as well, there was immediate trouble. The extra ganglion turned out to be a

lethal weapon. *Having two time-keepers sending out two completely different signals, the poor insect was thrown into turmoil. Its behavior became completely disorganized, and it soon developed acute stress symptoms, such as malignant tumors in the gut, and died.* (Watson, 1973, pp. 15-16)

DOUBLE MESSAGES

Imagine the implications of that! Even a #*@&^! *cockroach* will suffer consequences from incongruence! This experiment conducted by Janet Harker and reported in several scientific journals is tangible evidence of the adverse effect of the double message on a living organism. So it really is the "universal" that Virginia said it was. The appearance of the cockroach's malignant tumor also supports the idea of cancer being a kind of bodily schizophrenia.

I have seen, with my own eyes, the effect on psychotic children and adolescents of receiving double messages. One can watch, on the spot during the interview, how their speech becomes more confused as their anxiety levels rise. Virginia's intervention would be to give them permission to *verbalize* the anxiety and/or to *comment* on the process. (She got some of this from working with Gregory Bateson.) If the people are able to accept the possibility that they are sufficiently valuable as human beings for another person to want to effectively communicate with them, they may then move their system into harmony by verbally expressing–or acknowledging internally–the feeling that is raging or pouring throughout their body/mind/spirit system. This brings congruence.

Bringing one's system back into internal harmony means the person would not necessarily have to "develop acute stress symptoms . . . malignant tumors in the gut" and die a la the experimental cockroaches. Virginia said cancer comes from giving oneself a double-level message. Such a message results in there being no constructive place for the energy to then go.

I would never have thought a cockroach could grow a malignant tumor in its gut for *any* reason, let alone as a response to stress. I suppose I can assume that Watson and Harker wouldn't lie, but I think this is amazing information. Having to deal with double messages even kills *cockroaches!*

Many children grow up with double messages. One example, "Be Strong." In the case of oldest daughters, that can read as, "Take care of yourself and everybody around you." Such a girl, even knowing better on an intellectual level, can grow up with enormous trouble admitting to "weakness" or allowing herself to be emotionally vulnerable . . . all the time being, in fact, quite a sensitive person. Such a person, responding to the parental injunction to *behave as if* she were "strong"–while receiving the conflicting, overriding, message of fatigue from the body–puts herself in the double-message position by telling herself the lie that she "feels fine."

In growing up, children learn whatever they learn about reality from their parents. If a parent behaves as if you don't need something and you are a very little child, you think that must be fact–even though it flies in the face of your very organism's responses. A parental figure is as much survival mechanism for the very young child as are her/his own physiological instincts; a toddler would be in the same position as the cockroach with two timekeepers sending out different messages.

The parent who is unable to distinguish the needs of the child from her/his own sets the child up for schizophrenia, multiple personality, addiction, or cancer depending on the extent to which the parent is blind to the separate personhood of the child. There is evidence that the same is probably true for heart disease. It is a matter, using Virginia's concepts, of the parent not being able to appreciate and value the personhood of the new little person.

Babies are not "little vegetables"–they are little entities who have not yet developed the systems to communicate their internal experience. Nonetheless, the experience itself may be as sophisticated as yours or mine. It may not be organized, of course, but there is too much reporting of memories not to believe it is true. One client remembers her mother swearing at her when she stuck herself with a pin from the diaper. Another one remembers events from nine months to a year old. One young mother related, with appropriate horror, that her three-year-old son had reported sexual abuse by his baby-sitter. The abuse had occurred when he was 18 months old–too young to be able to describe it in words. By age three, he had the vocabulary to be able to tell her.

INHUMAN RULES

Virginia also talked a lot about the "inhuman rules" we have–those "shoulds" and "oughts" that keep us from clearly stating or even *knowing* our feelings. She invented the Family Reconstruction to take people on tours back in time to help them see where and how their *parent's* own shoulds and oughts perpetuated those rules. With new information about these "old learnings," a person is in a better position to make choices in reference to these rules.

I remember how startled I was back when I used to work in the state mental hospital and mental health system: to find myself able to help psychotic people stop their word salad by simply keying into what I was guessing their feeling to be, then helping them to identify it. Simply giving permission to people to openly state how they feel has enormous healing potential.

For Virginia, awareness was the key. The Family Reconstructions were all for the purpose of bringing information into conscious awareness.

Awareness of body response was both an end and a means to the end of "wholing" and learning to live out of wholeness. She would demonstrate how the four incongruent communication stances would feel in the body.

After a sequence of having participants sculpt their bodies into one of her four communication stances[5]:

> Any one of those things–when it comes to you–is telling you that your body is off-balance and, when you find it out, in some way the shoulds and oughts in your life are clashing and old triggers are coming back.
>
> [Asks two people to demonstrate the blaming-placating position]
>
> If that is what we have been doing, and I think we have, laws and everything else are into that one [the blaming-placating position]. Here we are, at this seminar becoming more fully human. We are steeped in this, the old, so it's not going to be an easy thing for you to say, "Well, I won't do this anymore." What we need to work on is the *awareness* of this. That's why when you are in your triads and one of you wants to go like that [extending blaming finger], you say, "Bless this for letting me know," instead of saying, "Oh, my god! Look at me. I'm doing the same old thing." This is the idea I would like for you to get into your heads, to be able to substitute "Oh, my god! ain't it awful?" for "Hey, I'm getting to be in touch. What's happening?" That is the part that saves us . . .
>
> . . . You can say nice, you can say nasty and even nice or nasty, and that [blaming-placating] is not a very whole picture. Now, what we're doing this whole month [of this seminar–August 1987] is going to be devoted to becoming aware. *The first thing is to let each of you now become aware of what your body feels like.* Close your eyes, take a breath, and now let your body expand so that it is comfortable and you're on your own feet. When you are on your own feet, you are following your own choice making . . .
>
> . . . What we are doing is living through thousands of years of acculturation about how we move with one another. Certainly western culture. We have been putting our energies into making the nasties a little bit not so nasty instead of going where we need to move which is a totally new place to being in touch and valuing . . . That's what the world needs at this time and that's what peace is about. (Satir, 1987, tape 3)

In this framework, we can understand how the body fits in the picture and how awareness (of one's whole person–body-mind-spirit) can lead to harmony with the self, with a partner, within a family, and on out into the greater community.

"... THE BODY IS TRYING TO SAY WHAT THE MOUTH CAN'T SAY..."

Virginia Satir

Virginia gave a two-week seminar in March 1972 that happened to fall just three weeks after her father's death. Her mother had died several years before–from cancer. The following excerpt is from one of her lectures following a demonstration:

Now let's look at the body responses. Here my medical friends kind of support me in this.

Let's look at the organs that are most affected. We think of a body as being a system that if any one part of it is affected–that means [other parts are affected]. There is a relationship to all the other parts. Have you noticed what happens to you when you have a corn? It isn't just that foot that has a corn on it, but it has a pain to it and the rest of your body gets into a problem. Everything is affected.

The organ affected first in placating is your belly–the whole digestive track, the nausea ...

Participant: Would you agree that most of the depressions go with placating?

Virginia: Yes, what's there to support feeling of self? All these others provide some out but this one doesn't.

You could call this the nauseating response–when I am saying what I don't feel.

Now here [blaming response] what are most affected are the tissues–the linings. Where is [participant]? This is what I want to get at with her and see what she's been doing to her linings that make her hands drawn. I may be successful, maybe not. I think there's something in that. The tissues get tight, and there's no flexibility. So explosions and all kinds of things like that are present.

Now here [super-reasonable] we get dryness. There are no juices here. The semen doesn't flow, the milk doesn't flow, the tears don't flow. Just dried up. So the problem here is no juice, no flexibility. And up here [placating] no boundaries.

Now we get down here [irrelevant] and what gets affected is the central nervous system–balance, dizziness. If your central nervous system isn't able to give you any kind of balance, all the rest of the parts of your body act accordingly.

What I have done now is to supply a base for psychosomatic medicine. When I said that the body is trying to say what the mouth can't say, in a squeeze, something has to happen.

I have a *theory of cancer.* I've spoken this to some of my friends and once spoke about this at a meeting. If we think about it for a minute, *cancer is wild, uncontrolled growth of a most energetic kind. That's where I start out. This is growth, and it's growth that's killing. What's causing the killing,* I ask myself? It has to be something in the person who won't allow something. What I see with the people that I work with *who have had terminal cancer* and some of those who didn't–none of this may fit any-way–first of all, *such a person has tremendous hopes, tremendous hopes and ambitions. Then somewhere along the line looks at the reality and says I can't do it. There's no point in hoping. But then the rules of that person are such that he can't allow himself to look like he did that, so now he has to make another rule that says he didn't do what he just did. And then to live as though he hasn't made the first decision.*

First I say to myself I can't do what I want to do. If [only] that, [alone], just happened you just get a depression. That would be like putting one line around your waist and squeezing–separating top and bottom. But then I have to behave as though I am still doing it. So now I have to put one around the neck.

Participant: Are you denying the loss of hope or are you denying the hope too?

Virginia: *You're denying the hope and the fact that you gave up hope. By this time, you never admitted that you even hoped. You live as though you didn't do either.*

If you understand what I am saying, it is like a double-level. First of all you tie one around here, which says I can't hope anymore. Then you tie one around here that says I didn't have the hope in the first place and I didn't even deny my hope because there wasn't any. I behave as though I'm hopeful and everything is going to be fine

Participant: Which does that go with?

Another participant: Number one.

Virginia: You start out here [number one–placating], then you end up here [number three–super-reasonable]. I watched my mother die of cancer and I knew this all the time. I knew what she was doing. When I was five years old, I knew my mother had tuned herself out of her ambitions-tuned herself completely off sexual joy with my father. I think it has a lot to do with validation in the sexual sphere. I'm now talking male and female, not just genital. I saw her literally behave as though I know she didn't feel. But it is more than just one lying.

You can just feel depressed. But then if you say to yourself I can't even do that, I have to behave cheery, then you send the body through an absolutely impossible situation. Where is that marvelous growth going to go?

Participant (who is an MD): You went through a progression that I missed–one to three.

Virginia: Do you know how many placaters are such very hard workers. Just tremendous. At some point, they give up, and it looks like they come over here [to super-reasonable]. But this is more than just a simple thing. After I got onto this and saw this over and over again, I had this couple come in and listened for a while and I heard. This was this woman's second marriage and she didn't see any other place for herself. I heard the things that said to me what I'm just now telling you about. Now it was all right, she was going to live her life this way. You would have to work very hard to hear the depressed part of it. I said to her when did you have your last physical. She told me a few months before. I said, "Listen, I can't tell you why–I did know why but I wasn't going to tell her because it was a hunch–I want you to go for a physical to a good doctor tomorrow." That was Tuesday. On Friday she had her right breast removed. It was there. You can smell this kind of stuff.

. . . This is not refined as a mathematical model. But you can begin as you hear this. It's kind of like for me the skeleton and how it gets fleshed in and how it relates. But I do know the physical response that seems to be very obvious in relation to this. (1972 Aruba tape transcript, p. 289)

These clinical observations Virginia made during her fifty-plus years of experience obviously have profound implications for cancer patients and for therapists who work with cancer patients.

VIRGINIA ON WHOLENESS: BODY, MIND, AND SOUL TOGETHER

Process More Important than Content

Virginia kept using "river of life" imagery: all of life is process.

Virginia knew that events, human interaction, and human dynamics do not exist in discrete pieces. She thought and taught in terms of wholeness, demonstrating the importance of sensory awareness. We make our connections with each other through use of our sensory apparatus, and we make sense of our surroundings through those same sense organs.

She enjoyed using humor and would use a play on words to carry her meaning: our "holes" (our sense organs), wholeness, "holey-ness" (our aware use of our sensory input), and holiness. In other words, use your senses to give you more extensive information about your own inner processes as well as those of your partner or family member. This aware use of senses is one aspect of "wholeness." Use of intellect, alone, is an illusion. We are always responding to non-verbal body cues. Two people connect via these "holes." Each human being is a unique creation in the universe; when two such beings meet, this is a spiritual event–therefore, holiness born of "holey-ness."

In the Satir Model, the good therapist would (1) cultivate sensory aware- ness, (2) understand that information transmits affectively as well as cogni- tively, and (3) value every other human being as that utterly unique creation that he or she is.

Wholeness is looking at people, in their various contexts, as parts of an ongoing process–the continual flow of living.

SELF MANDALA

Satir looks to unify elements of self through a series of questions:

> . . . My picture: If . . . all these parts were known to us and accepted by us, we would have a *spiral of all these things together* . . .
>
> . . . We would never forget that they're all connected to something else. So that the eight questions I would ask myself when something happens is (1) Where am I in my feeling of love for my life-force? [spiritual] (2) Where am I in terms of what I've been eating? [nutrition- al] (3) Where am I in terms of what I've been thinking? [intellectual] (4) What I have been feeling? [emotional] (5) What my *body* is doing? [physical and sensual](6) What have been my interactions with people? [interactional].[6]
>
> And I could begin to take a self-administered inventory . . . help . . . me . . . be where I was. Add up negative use of all that and you get stress which kills. That is what stress is about. These things [the eight] don't work harmoniously. Why? There is a thought I can't bear, there's a situation I don't want the way that it is, or whatever. (Banmen and Satir, 1983, pp. 270-271)

She often used herself as example:

> Last week one day–I have never in my awareness had an allergy. Last week my nose ran and I had no idea where that all came from, but I had no feelings about a cold, *My first time having an allergy.* I got an allergy pill–the best, I thought, to do from [participant X] and it all cleared up. I still don't know what that was. I'll be interested to know how that all happened, but for me now, it's an academic thing. But I did have it . . . so I wouldn't think only about the pollen that was around, I began to think on all these eight levels. Where was I? (Banmen and Satir, 1983, p. 269)

In her lecture, she is giving some history about the inattention by therapists to these eight factors which are all, in her words, "universal personal resources" in the spiral of the "self mandala" (1983, p. 258): (1) the body, the physical; (2) the intellectual; (3) the emotional; (4) the sensual; (5) the interactional; (6) the nutritional; (7) the contextual; (8) the spiritual–the life-force.

> Historically, "we put the spiritual in the hands of religion," permitted only the people in the performing arts to make use of the sensual (learn about their voice, etc.), behaved as though the contextual did not exist, ignored the implications of the nutritional, only paid attention to the interactional in terms of bad behavior, related the emotional to morality, and left the physical and the intellectual in the hands of physicians and teachers respectively. "And none of those people spoke to each other." (pp. 260-261)

INGREDIENTS OF AN INTERACTION

She also says about the interactional, ". . . my ingredients of an interaction . . . There is nothing written anywhere in the world [in 1983] about that. I was the first one to put this together, but that wasn't because the information wasn't there but nobody paid any attention to it" (p. 260).

The Ingredients of an Interaction explores two factors that influence our patterns of interacting:

1. The family rules we follow for processing information.
2. Our coping style [placating, blaming, super-reasonable, or irrelevant], which reflects our self-worth and gives us the basis for how we hear, feel, react, defend, and comment. (Satir, 1991, p. 122)

FULL PERSONHOOD

Virginia Satir worked hard to instill the concept of wholeness in her trainees. Her work was always in terms of body-mind-soul, and she was among the early pioneers in bringing psychotherapy out of "intellect only" and into pursuing the goal of full personhood of both client and therapist.

NOTES

1. Readers should note: all cited lectures are taken out of context. They were interspersed between exercises and live demonstrations–all part of one of the Avanta Process Community Meetings at Crested Butte, Colorado, 1981-1987.
2. Virginia is referring to her system of identifying incongruent responses: blaming, placating or self-deprecating, super-reasonable, and irrelevant (Satir, 1991).

3. Super-reasonable stance: behaving as if the human beings involved do not matter, that only the task or intellectual content matters.

4. Virginia Satir strongly objected to the concept of "techniques" in regard to her work. Instead, she preferred the word "vehicle"–a means of moving toward a mutual goal rather than an act she would be performing.

5. Stress ballet–term Virginia used to describe the motions through which a given dyad would go, shifting among the four incongruent communication styles in response to stress. A person might start out with placation and rise to her/his feet, so to speak, and launch into blaming, then resort to the robot-like stance of super-reasonable behavior or irrelevant behavior–then change again. Changes would often be in response to the dyad partner's given stance.

6. This last identification in "The Self Mandala" between interaction and context is inherent: human "context" is always "interactions." However, the contextual refers to the broad "here and now" of the current greater outer reality containing any given human interaction (Satir, 1991, pp. 274-277).

REFERENCES

Brothers, B.J. (1987). "Independence" *avoids* intimacy: Avoidance of intimacy kills. *Voices: The Art and Science of Psychotherapy, 21* (Spring), 10-23.

Brothers, B.J. (1989). The cancer patient is the self-contained patient. In E. Mark Stern (Ed.), *The self-contained patient* (pp. 227-241). Binghamton, NY: The Haworth Press, Inc.

Brothers, B.J. (2000). Virginia Satir. In M. Suhd (Ed.), *Virginia Satir: Her life and circle of influence*. Mountain View, CA: Science and Behavior Books.

Harker, J.E. (1954). Diurnal rhythms in *Periplaneta americana* L. *Nature, 173,* 689.

Harker, J.E. (1956). Factors controlling the diurnal rhythms of activity in *Periplaneta americana* L. *Journal of Experimental Biology, 33*: 224.

Harker, J.E. (1958). Diurnal rhythms in the animal kingdom. *Biological Reviews, 33,* 1.

Satir, V. (1972). Presentation at a seminar on Aruba (Cassette recordings transcript). Falls Church, VA: Lori Gordon, PAIRS Foundation (3705 South George Mason Drive, #C35; 22041).

Satir, V., & Banmen, J. (1983). *Virginia Satir verbatim 1984* (Transcript of the Process Community III in Crested Butte, CO). North Delta, BC, Canada: Delta Psychological Services (11213 Canyon Crescent; V4E2R6).

Satir, V. (1987). Audiotaped presentations at Avanta Process Community VII, Module I, in Crested Butte, CO. Blue Moon Cassettes, recordings 5. Santa Barbara, CA: Virginia Satir Archives, Special Collection, Davison Library, University of California.

Satir, V. (1991). *The Satir model*. Palo Alto, CA: Science and Behavior Books.

Watson, L. (1973). *Supernature*. Garden City, NY: Anchor Press/Doubleday.

Grounding in Couples
Core Energetic Therapy

Mary J. Giuffra

SUMMARY. This article explores the Theory of Grounding as an important component of Couples Therapy. Therapeutic techniques which physically ground partners in their bodies are discussed and contraindications highlighted.

In order to hear one another during times of increased conflict and intense emotionality, partners are taught skills which they practice for use during stressful times. Therapists can also employ grounding techniques, particularly with couples who trigger their reactivity. The underpinning of grounding in Core Energetic Therapy is described. *[Article copies available for a fee*

Mary J. Giuffra, PhD, CS, CFT, FAAN, is a Fellow of the American Academy of Nursing, Certified Clinical Specialist in Psychiatric Mental Health Nursing, Certified Sex Educator and Counselor, Certified Family and Couples Therapist, and Certified Core Energetic Therapist. She is Vice-President of The United States Association for Body Psychotherapy. She was a tenured professor at New York University where she received MA and PhD degrees and at College of Mount St. Vincent where she founded BS and MS nursing programs and was awarded an honorary Doctorate in Humane Letters. She was on the Editorial Board of the *Journal of Professional Nursing* published by the American Association of Colleges of Nursing. She was a faculty member and supervisor at The Center for Family Learning for 14 years and is currently Director of Research at the Institute for Core Energetics. She has been in private practice for 20 years, the last 11 years on a full-time basis.

The author of numerous articles and book chapters on couples and family therapy, culture and its impact on couple dynamics, physical illness, and the family, she has presented research findings on the impact of death on the family system. She has served as an alternate delegate to the United Nations for non-governmental organizations. Currently, she is Governor of Lawrence Hospital and Chair of the Board at Home Nursing Association of Westchester, Jansen Memorial Hospice and The Bereavement Center of Westchester.

[Haworth co-indexing entry note]: "Grounding in Couples Core Energetic Therapy." Giuffra, Mary J. Co-published simultaneously in *Journal of Couples Therapy* (The Haworth Press, Inc.) Vol. 10, No. 2, 2001, pp. 17-23; and: *Couples and Body Therapy* (ed: Barbara Jo Brothers) The Haworth Press, Inc., 2001, pp. 17-23. Single or multiple copies of this article are available for a fee from The Haworth Document Delivery Service [1-800-342-9678, 9:00 a.m. - 5:00 p.m. (EST). E-mail address: getinfo@haworthpressinc.com].

17

KEYWORDS. Grounding techniques, body consciousness, couples therapy

"The most brilliant and philosophically subtle therapy in the world will have no impact on a couple not grounded in their own bodies to hear it," concludes John Gottman, who has physiologically monitored the emotions, behaviors, and hormones of thousands of married couples in his Research Lab at the University of Washington.

As a former obstetric and pediatric nurse, I knew how important touch and physical support were in grounding people. However, my couples and family training was geared to sitting with and talking to clients. A shake of the hand at the beginning or end of a session complemented physical sculpting of a family or the inevitable Genogram on a flipchart, the trademark of Bowenian family therapists.

While working with hundreds of couples and participating in clinical research projects to study marriages, I learned a great deal about myself and about them. Many relationships thrived and others fell by the wayside. Each partner left knowing a good deal more about his or her extended family and some of the triangular patterns that kept repeating over the generations. Intense emotionality lessened. Regardless of whether the partners stayed together or chose to split, a little more reason generally prevailed. Partnership and companionship tended to improve and sometimes romance reblossomed.

Nevertheless, I often sensed that two components were missing, spirituality and the body. Consequently, I did further training in addictions and in spiritual psychology and mythology. For couples in twelve step programs, who were recovering from the addictive process, spirituality was an essential aspect of their healing. Spirituality became part of therapy. I became more integrated as a therapist.

But the grounding that comes from deeply connecting with one's body, therapeutically eluded me until I met John Pierrakos, the founder of Core Energetic Evolutionary Therapy. A forthright, intelligent, and big-hearted man with a soft Greek accent, John's mantra was: "But what about the body."

A psychiatrist whose mentor was Wilhelm Reich, Pierrakos co-founded Bioenergetics with Alexander Lowen. Intense focus on physical exercise and specific movements which release physical blocks and open breathing free clients to express their inner truth from a very grounded, conscious, and energetic place.

With a Bowenian background in biology and evolution, I wondered if somehow dendrites in the brain were expanding as a result of people's inhabiting their bodies more fully. Perhaps this was an avenue to fuller use of the brain. Was guided physical movement a way to enhance evolution? Occupational and physical therapists work with people who have developmental deficits. Guided physical movements help reconnect brain and body. From this grounded place, it seemed as if patterns that repeated over generations were experienced physically as well as studied intellectually. This John Pierrakos was on to something. I wanted to know more.

I called John for a session and was asked to write a letter explaining my life and describing what I hoped to achieve in Core Energetic Therapy. Murray Bowen and the managed care companies would love his appeal to reason and request for therapeutic outcomes. Since life was going well, my goals were to increase consciousness on a deeper and more physical level and to be receptive to the wondrous world surrounding me. I understood that Pierrakos had expanded from Bioenergetics to include spirituality and positive intentionality as well as the body, mind, and emotions. He incorporated the spiritual principles of the Pathwork Guide Lectures and founded Core Energetics.

I felt such a sense of completeness. Finally, the wholeness that I had theorized about was becoming a practical reality. David Boehm and the "new physics" with its premise that everything is interconnected and in dynamic flux dovetailed nicely with Core Energetics. Consciousness and energy are the underpinnings from which Core Energetic therapists approach their clients.

Following two years of therapy with Pierrakos, I decided to join the Core Energetic training program. I hoped to learn some techniques which could be integrated into my couples and family practice. After the second year, I was intrigued. There was more going on here than techniques. We were working with energy fields and deep transformation was taking place. My practice was blooming.

An anxious or depressed couple would come for a session, and, by the time they left, they would not only feel more grounded and able to cope, they would also have physical skills they could employ at home. Their bodies began to change, their voices and breathing opened. Their relationships improved or they ended them. In addition to its central focus on physical work, the emphasis on opening one's heart and developing the ability to love and feel pleasure distinguishes Core Energetics from other therapies.

Five more years of Core training, therapy, and supervision have given me a tremendous comfort level in working with couples. I always had an intellectual understanding of the systems dynamics, but the sense of emotional ease and grounding that I now experience is different. I can feel energetic changes in the couple as we do the work. At the same time, my mental clarity is more acute.

Tuning into the spiritual dimension of a couples' life has added richness to the work and to my life. From the client who identifies as an avowed atheist yet experiences a deep connection with nature, to the orthodox person who follows ancient rituals, my life has become fuller. Couples tell me that they feel seen and honored.

At a recent birthday celebration for the founder of the Institute where I did my couples and family training, and served on the faculty for many years, colleagues commented on how alive and well I looked. Perhaps the fountain of youth is the flow of energy that comes from grounding to mother earth, releasing energetic blocks, opening the heart, and becoming conscious of how genetic and environmental programming limit our freedom to receive life.

I want to share some Core Energetic grounding techniques that are useful for a couples therapist. Use clinical judgement and try them out as you deem appropriate. Study the results. Compare outcomes for couples who use the skills at home with couples who do not. I would appreciate your sharing thoughts and findings with me.

An experienced therapist knows that techniques are not the heart of therapy. As Orlinsky noted in the fourth edition of the *Handbook of Psychiatry and Behavior Change*, "The quality of the patient's participation in therapy stands out as the most important determinant of outcome."

As the research cited earlier in the article highlights, grounding in the body is essential if couples are to hear each other or the therapist. Ground couples early in the session. Teach them how to ground at home, especially before, during, and after conflicts. In a perfect world, a mindful person is grounded in her/his body at every moment of waking life.

This would be true paradise since we humans withdraw into our heads at the least stress. We hold our breath and set the wheels of the intellect in motion as an attempt to feel in control of those intense feelings. Programming from our evolutionary and cultural heritage has been changed by the familial, educational, and social environments in which we developed. Some of us "space-out" and leave our bodies. Others of us lash out in ungrounded aggression. There are times when we withdraw our energetic grounding from mother earth and helplessly expect others to make us feel more comfortable.

Early on, Murray Bowen theorized that the differentiated person could be in contact with intense emotionality (in the body) and mentally clear at the same moment. Grounding life energies to the earth is a road to simultaneity of intense emotional, mental, and spiritual clarity.

Before plugging a highly charged appliance into a socket, a ground is needed to discharge excess electrons into the earth. We know that human beings are conductors of electricity. Furthermore, therapists experience charged couples sessions, where the ungrounded energy is palpable. Yet, very simple techniques can ground a couple.

Gottman talks about the flooding response in couples where their minds are clouded by the chemicals discharged into the body under extreme stress. However, it is also true that one couple's stressor is another couple's challenge. Our biological, familial, sociocultural, educational and environmental programming, beliefs, and stories predispose us to see situations as crises rather than as opportunities for growth. Flooding is often an outcome.

A simple yet very grounding technique is to make eye-to-eye contact. If possible, have the clients stand up on their feet. Unless they have been sexually abused or are touch avoidant, take their hands and have them make eye contact with you or with each other, although that may be tricky if there is a lot of reactivity between them. It will increase the emotional flooding unless they can stay grounded. In that case, the therapist can hold each of their hands and leave them physically separated.

When the therapist is grounded, she need not worry about getting caught in triangles. Triangles are a result of grounding our energies in another person instead of the earth. Although reactivity is human, and therapists are not immune from triangular communication, frequent monitoring of our energetic connection to the earth is invaluable for couples therapists.

Another technique is simply to stand up and bend one's knees, ever so slightly. As anyone who has skied a steep mountain will attest, the steeper the hill, the closer you bend your knees to the ground. When anxious, the touch of mother earth is a haven. Look at a dog or cat when they sense danger. The animal crouches closer to the ground before they pounce. It is the ungrounded cat who leaps away in terror.

Sometimes you can conduct an entire session where both of the partners are standing up with their knees slightly bent. Locking one's knees can be equated to cutting off energy at the knees. Clients who lock knees can be taught to soften them. They will feel more grounded but they will also feel more. As children we learn that locking our knees cuts off feelings. In the past, it may have served a useful purpose in avoiding pain that we were unequipped to handle. Therapy provides more creative options for dealing with that pain.

Perhaps as therapists, we can graduate from the couch to the chair and finally to our own two feet. At the start of a session, I often have a couple take off shoes and press their feet to the floor, first walking on heels, and then on the balls of their feet. Shake the ankles in a circular motion, clockwise and then counter-clockwise. Do the same with the knees and then with the hips; first do one leg and then the other. Next I have clients stretch as if they are taking something from the sky and pulling it down to earth. As I am writing this, I can imagine my readers saying, "This is weird." If you are hesitant, try it on yourself and observe. See if you feel more present and grounded as you read the rest of the article.

For a particularly negative and resistant couple, you can have them stamp their feet and keep repeating, "No, No, No!" In this way, you are honoring their feelings, grounding them, and providing an opportunity to release some of their tension. They will be more open to the work of the session.

Of course, clinical judgement is an essential component in the decision to apply any technique with a couple. Your comfort level and that of the client are paramount. If the therapist is not comfortable using a technique, the client will feel unsafe. Emotional or physical handicaps can also limit the appropriateness of these techniques.

In an emergency, when someone is in the throes of severe emotional flooding, have them place their back to the wall and gradually slide down the wall until the knees are directly over the ankles. Physical trainers and athletes know that extending the knees beyond the ankles puts undue stress on the knees. This is a useful technique but is only to be used in an emergency as it can make the person feel very vulnerable.

Just working in a garden grounds people. Having a client sift sand or earth through their fingers can help bring them into their bodies. I have a small Zen garden in the office for this purpose. Walking barefoot on sand, earth, or grass is useful when they are at home.

After asking for permission to touch, a basic requirement for all Core Energetic Therapy, place the palm of the hand on the center of the client's back. This is an extremely grounding and supportive move that can continue as a client explores his process. In the case of a couple, you may gently support each of them. A hand on the shoulder is another grounding move that people do instinctively.

In some states, therapists are not permitted to touch clients. In that case, teach the couple some of the grounding moves. Demonstrate by moving your feet and legs. Monitor clients as they perform these exercises. Eye-to-eye contact is always a possibility.

In family therapy, we say that if an individual is suicidal or depressed, bring in the family. Although we do not call it grounding, that is what it is. The reason it is so stressful to be in the presence of extended family is that we become grounded. A twelve step meeting can be grounding for someone in recovery from an addiction.

The downside is that when you become grounded, you feel. Why would anyone leave this marvelous body to attend to a mechanical intellect or to disassociate, if they were not uncomfortable feeling the messages and sensations of body and emotions. We develop various defenses to keep us ungrounded and unfeeling.

This article does not begin to touch the depth of Core Energetic Evolutionary Therapy. It is simply an attempt to come back to the family of couples and family therapy and share some of the findings from my journey. I believe that the energy field created by the presence of a conscious, open, flowing therapist provides an environment in which healing takes place.

My earliest mentor at New York University, Martha Rogers, taught that outcomes were a result of the "individual interacting with the environment, changing and being changed." Since we are the couple's therapeutic environment, the more present we are to ourselves and the more grounded in our bodies, the more fully we can teach them to relate from a centered place. Note John Gottman's research findings from his rigorous study of thousands of couples: "The most brilliant and philosophically subtle therapy in the world will have no effect on a couple not grounded in their own bodies to hear it."

BIBLIOGRAPHY

Bowen, M. *Family Therapy in Clinical Practice.* Jason Aronson Inc., New York & London, 1978.

Cooper, G. "Much Ado About Marital Therapy." *The Networker*, May-June 1998, pp. 13-14.

Gottman, J. *Why Marriages Succeed or Fail.* Fireside Book, Simon & Schuster. New York, London, Toronto, Tokyo, Singapore, 1994.

Pierrakos, J. *Eros, Love and Sex.* Life Rhythm Press, Mendocino, CA, 1998.

Core Energetic Couples Therapy:
An Integrated Approach

Karyne B. Wilner

SUMMARY. Core energetics is a method of psychotherapy that seeks the integration of all aspects of humanity: the emotional, physical, mental, and spiritual. Based on a deep understanding of the ways in which energy and consciousness work together, the therapy, developed by John C. Pierrakos, MD, invites couples to experience their inner truth and to identify their universal life goals and core feelings. Core energetics emphasizes wholeness and unification without loss of individuation for the couple. This article describes core energetics as it is used in couples work; the theory, therapeutic stance, methods of diagnosis, and energetic techniques are discussed, as well as the focus on sexuality and spirituality. *[Article copies available for a fee from The Haworth Document Delivery Service: 1-800-342-9678. E-mail address: <getinfo@haworthpressinc. com> Website: <http://www.HaworthPress.com> © 2001 by The Haworth Press, Inc. All rights reserved.]*

KEYWORDS. Couples therapy, energy therapy, spirituality, body/mind, relationship therapy

Karyne B. Wilner, MA, is a Licensed Psychologist in Philadelphia, PA. She is Director of the Delaware Valley Core Energetics Center which conducts individual, couples, and group therapy as well as training workshops. In the past, she has directed Humanistic Interactional Associates, a private psychotherapy practice, and the Drexel University Counseling Center. Currently, she is a doctoral candidate in psychology at Philadelphia College of Osteopathic Medicine.

Karyne is very involved with Core Energetics worldwide. As International Coordinator and Director of Education, she is involved with many adminisrative functions. Her teaching takes her to Brazil, where she is Director of the Brazil Core Energetic program, and to other countries, such as Germany, Switzerland, Italy, Canada, and Mexico.

[Haworth co-indexing entry note]: "Core Energetic Couples Therapy: An Integrated Approach." Wilner, Karyne B. Co-published simultaneously in *Journal of Couples Therapy* (The Haworth Press, Inc.) Vol. 10, No. 2, 2001, pp. 25-34; and: *Couples and Body Therapy* (ed: Barbara Jo Brothers) The Haworth Press, Inc., 2001, pp. 25-34. Single or multiple copies of this article are available for a fee from The Haworth Document Delivery Service [1-800-342-9678, 9:00 a.m. - 5:00 p.m. (EST). E-mail address: getinfo@ haworthpressinc.com].

25

Core energetics is a method of psychotherapy that seeks the integration of all aspects of humanity–the emotional, physical, mental, and spiritual. Based on a deep understanding of the ways in which energy and consciousness work together, the therapy invites clients to experience their inner truth and to identify their universal life goals and core feelings. John C. Pierrakos, MD, created core energetics in the 1970s, integrating teachings from his studies with Wilhelm Reich and his collaboration with Alexander Lowen, with whom he developed bioenergetics) into a spiritual model inspired by Eva Pierrakos. This article describes core energetics as it is used in couples work; the theory, therapeutic stance, methods of diagnosis, and energetic techniques are discussed, as well as the focus on sexuality and spirituality.

Core energetic therapists work with couples using expressive exercises, deep breathing exercises, and therapeutic touch in order to release energy blockages and facilitate the expression of feelings. They also employ spiritual and cognitive technologies to help couples reveal their truth, eliminate irrational beliefs, experience unity within themselves, and share love and pleasure at deeper levels. The body, along with the clinical interview, is the instrument of diagnosis. Bodies, which are shaped by energetic flow and blockage, as well as by heredity, provide the therapist with insight into each client's life history and each couple's pattern of interaction.

THEORETICAL POSITION

Many couples who call for therapy are unaware of the powerful unconscious dynamics that have affected their personalities and that have consequences for their relationships. In therapy, they learn that early relationships with their parents, heredity, the environment, and the culture have worked together to mold their bodies and create their character structures and personalities. The therapist describes this developmental process, explaining that, at birth, the child brings to the planet the soul's capacity for beauty, creativity, faith, truth, and love (Pierrakos, 1990). This is the essence of the higher self. Also at birth, the physical body provides the organism with tools to help it protect itself, such as the ability to express anger, fear, rage, and terror. This automatic response to threat, known as the fight or flight response, is often frustrated by societal norms. Early in life children are taught that negative feelings are not to be tolerated and that they should expect some form of punishment if they are expressed. In reaction, strong affect is hidden, repressed, and distorted in the body. The emotions are replaced by the mask self, a false, but socially acceptable self, which is composed of chronic tensions, projections, rationalizations, and diminished feeling states.

The suppression of negative affect and the substitution of the mask self in its place facilitates survival, but causes energy dysfunction, a hardening of the musculature, a suppression of physical sensation and feeling, distorted behavior, and dysfunctional coping mechanisms. Children grow into adulthood, acting and reacting from their defenses, separated from the beauty of their true selves. In order to resolve these problems, couples are encouraged to release energetic blocks, break through their mask selves, express their lower selves, and connect with their natural gifts and their deepest truth, the source of creativity and universal love, their higher selves.

The most important core energetic principle taught to couples is "the will to love" (Pierrakos, 1997). Love is regarded as more than a feeling and as more than an erotic force. It is viewed as a mindset, combining loving thoughts toward the other with positive actions. Pierrakos explains that love "is guided by and motivated by intelligence." It is impossible to love the partner without using the will. When the will of one or both partners is dysfunctional, a primary goal of the therapy is to transform it and bring it into a more balanced energetic state. This is necessary in cases where one or both wills are overly strong, controlling, and demanding or where one or both wills are passive, lacking initiative, and depressed. Often a person with an overly strong will is married to a person with an undeveloped will, leading to resentment and unhappiness in both partners. While one partner feels burdened with too much responsibility, the other experiences a loss of freedom after submitting to the partner's need for control. In one such case, the male came to me for help because his fiancée of five years left the relationship. He explained that he could not understand her behavior, because he had moved her into his house and had given her his dental practice to manage. When asked, he confided that they had not married because he could not afford to give her the thirty thousand dollar wedding he assumed she wanted. Although she never verbalized how she felt about having "no say" in the relationship, she finally left. Often people with underdeveloped wills speak with behavior rather than words, but only when pushed to the brink.

In some couples, the will to love is diminished due to past rejections, which lead to the fear of getting hurt again, and, in others, it is diminished by narcissistic impulses, such as a lack of empathy and an exaggerated sense of one's own importance. Other couples demonstrate the desire to love, but lack the skills to initiate the required actions. They may need help in learning communications skills, assertiveness skills, energetic skills, and sexual skills which emphasize reaching out, receiving, giving, expressing emotion, and making contact, both verbally and physically (Beck & Freeman, 1990; Pierrakos, 1990).

Another theory that is useful for work with couples, concerns the repetition of childhood hurts, an unconscious effort to heal wounds from the past. Pathwork Lecture, Number 73, *The Compulsion to Recreate and Overcome Childhood Hurts* (Broch, 1960) illustrates this theory and can be assigned to the couple to read. Points to be discussed in session include: (1) the infant's unrealistic desire to be loved exclusively, (2) the belief that if needs were not filled by one's parents, they should be filled later in life by a relationship partner, (3) the illusion that if the initial deprivation is reproduced, the consequences will be different when reenacted, and (4) the evidence that people choose life partners who have personality aspects similar to or suggestive of the frustrating parent. Healing in terms of these issues occurs when the partners stop blaming each other for their unfulfilled needs. In addition, they must risk experiencing the longing and hurt in relationship to their families of origin and learn to take responsibility for fulfilling their individual needs, rather than relying on the relationship partner to do so.

In one such couple who came for therapy, the wife was extremely critical, sarcastic, and punitive toward her husband when he made any purchase, small or large. In response, he hated her secretly, walking "on eggshells" in her presence, and hiding bills and receipts. Sharing her family history, she related that her father, who she loved, was a gambler. The family finances were so reduced due to her father's addiction that her parents were forced to sell their house and live with relatives. Her mother was always working and extremely bitter and unhappy. Unconsciously, she recreated in her marital relationship the psychological atmosphere in which she had been raised. Her attitude toward her husband, like that toward her original family, was one of distrust and suspicion. She responded to her husband with accusation and blame, even though there were no facts to support her suppositions. The resolution to their marital difficulties began with the experience of the original pain and betrayal by both partners in relation to their early histories. The husband also brought family of origin material to the marriage. Because he was abused as a child by his oldest sister, he recreated this situation with his wife.

Other therapeutic issues that core energetics couples therapists emphasize are taken from the field of family therapy. These include indirect loyalties and destructive entitlement (Zuk & Boszormenyi-Nagy, 1969), the role of the triangle when children or parents are involved, the process of individuation versus enmeshment (Glick, Clarkin, & Kessler, 1987), and the family as a system (Minuchin & Fishman, 1981). In addition, the following are all essential to the therapeutic process with couples: attaining a balance between giving and receiving; using the combined forces of reason, will, and emotion in decision making; releasing suppressed anger in a safe and supportive atmosphere; and opening the heart. Couples are taught that an energy flow, particularly when it is guided by the heart, creates an atmosphere of pleasure, joy, and fulfillment in the relationship. Relationships based on an energy flow lead to mutual attraction, sharing, companionship, and intellectual stimulation, rather than to disappointment, distancing, resentment, and blame.

THERAPEUTIC APPLICATION

In core energetic couples therapy, the therapist's stance is important. The spiritual nature of the therapy requires that therapists be in their higher selves when meeting their clients. This necessitates being in a state of truth, displaying congruity between feelings and actions, receiving clients without judgment or criticism, and maintaining contact with one's spiritual center. The therapist is sincere, genuine, open, and willing to collaborate with the client to find a solution to the problem which is presented. Therapists use the energy of their hearts to make contact, build rapport, and plan appropriate interventions. Continually working on themselves, core energetic therapists engage in deep breathing, energetic exercises, and meditation or prayer prior to the therapy session. When the session begins, they quietly center themselves and observe the higher selves of the clients. Although the clients' mask states are usually more visible than their higher selves, a few seconds are taken in order to view the underlying beauty of these people who have called for help.

It is also helpful to conduct a clinical interview in person, rather than having clients fill out forms in the waiting room. It is my belief that rapport building occurs while the history is being taken. When the therapist is asking questions and writing down answers, safety is being established. Clients are provided with an opportunity to look the therapist over without being observed themselves. The structure of the interview also helps to place boundaries around difficult topics, so that they are approached slowly with the therapist in control of the situation. The structured interview gives the couple an opportunity to hear each other's history in an objective and unemotional atmosphere. One person can listen to material concerning the other's past without offering judgment or criticism. I have observed that even in couples married many years, one or both is often surprised by some of the material that is elicited. Topics covered in the written assessment include background information concerning: education, work life, family of origin, marital status, children, health, addictions, sexual relationships, prior therapy, religion, and suicide.

After the presenting problem is heard, core energetics is introduced as a therapeutic model. One of the first therapeutic issues involves identification and analysis of each person's higher self, lower self, and mask self. There are several reasons this activity is suggested in the earliest stage of the therapy. First, clients learn that a spiritual self is a significant aspect of this form of psychotherapy. Secondly, an exploration of these three personality levels provides another form of diagnosis and assessment for the therapist to utilize. The presentation of the mask self often helps to identify personality disorders, such as narcissistic, avoidant, and borderline personalities, as well as Axis I diagnoses, such as depression and anxiety. Finally, an introduction to the higher self, lower self, and mask self emphasizes the unacceptability of blame. Blame, which is a mask issue, hides underlying feelings of rage and anger. A couple must be taught to go beyond the desire to blame the other and instead take responsibility, each for his or her own disappointment, frustration, hurt, pain, and anger.

A standard method for eliciting these personality aspects is "the three pillow exercise" (Pierrakos, 1986). Different pillows are chosen by the person working to represent the mask, lower self, and higher self. Sitting on one of the pillows and facing the other partner, honest feelings are expressed. For example, the mask self would judge, saying: "you are impossible to live with, you don't care about me or the kids, you are selfish and only you matter." The lower self would say in a loud, menacing tone of voice with matching facial expression: " I hate you. I will hurt you. I will make your life miserable and withhold my love whenever possible." Finally, the higher self might say: "You are a very special person. You supported me through Mom's death and were at my side the entire time, and I love you for that." Usually, clients must speak from the mask and lower self, before they are able to voice the higher self sincerely. Both people should have the opportunity to exhibit all three personality states during the session. After months of hearing blame and criticism, the expression of clear forms of anger and love begins to transform the relationship.

An energy assessment, which involves observation and analysis of posture, muscular tension, facial expression, aura level, and chakra energy, is also conducted during the initial phase of treatment. The couple is asked to bring or wear bathing suits to the session for the assessment, which, similar to the history taking session, helps each partner learn new material about the other. While one partner listens, the therapist explains the energy patterns observed in the other's body. Wilhelm Reich (1950) taught that the body exhibits the frozen history of a person. Using strategies passed down from Reich, and learned from Pierrakos (1990), the therapist is able to attain information about childhood development that may have been missed during the verbal assessment.

The clients' energetic patterns are identified as fragmented, undercharged, overcharged, upwardly displaced, or rigidified (Lowen, 1958; Pierrakos, 1990). Observed energetic dysfunctions provide the therapist with information about particular problems in living, wounds received as a child, and unresolved material from the family of origin. For instance, the schizoid defense, which develops in relationship to a wound prior to six months of age, is characterized by fragmented energy, a weak ego, and a feeling of nonexistence. Feelings of abandonment plague the person who develops an oral, energetically undercharged defense in response to a wound between six months and one-and-a-half years of age. A masochistic, energetically overcharged wounding occurs between two and three years of age and involves intrusive parenting, attachment, and independence issues. Parenting that wavers chaotically between seductiveness and hostility, when directed at a child age three to five, results in a psychopathic defense and an upward displacement of energy in the body. Finally, the rigid defense is characterized by mechanical and unemotional energetic functioning, resulting from a wound received during the oedipal stage, ages four to seven.

Each of these character defenses is a normal reaction to undesirable circumstances. Although the defenses allow the child to survive, they decrease the adult's ability to function and cope in healthy ways. The information from the energy analysis can also be used to identify specific problems in the relationship with which each couple must cope. For instance, a partner with an upper displacement of energy has little trust and, therefore, will try to control most situations in order to regulate their outcome. If that person is married to someone with a similar upper displacement, many power battles will occur. Both people need to ground their energy and learn to surrender, compromise, and trust.

Following the initial assessment and rapport building phase of the therapy, the work phase begins when many couples begin to confront their masks. Mask behaviors are utilized to avoid facing lower self feelings hidden beneath the mask. The mask allows clients to remain in denial about their underlying cruelty and destructive urges. Typical masks seen in couples therapy include: the absent, unavailable partner; the needy, dependent partner; the sweet, superficially pleasant partner who hides passive aggressive behavior, such as "I will never give it to you"; the controlling partner; the perfectionist, achievement oriented partner; the alcoholic or emotionally abusive partner; and the partner who lusts after others and engages in affairs.

Once the masks are identified and confronted, the underlying lower self layer is revealed. Both individuals are taught to release negativity toward each other in a safe and supportive way. Activities may involve growling at each other, pushing against each other and saying "no," engaging in a tug of war or a pillow fight, and standing across from each other on either side of a bed wielding encounter bats or tennis rackets and hitting, while making primitive and violent sounds. As this negativity is released, energy held in the body discharges and begins to flow. It is important to show the couple how to bring this newly released energy down toward the ground, because energy moving up toward the head can result in headaches, neck tension, or other unpleasant sensations. In addition, the partners should help each other with the grounding exercises that are assigned as homework.

In addition to engaging in lower self work toward each other, partners should work with their lower selves to resolve family-of-origin issues. If transference is not addressed in the couples therapy, it is probable that unfinished business with the mother or the father will continue to be projected onto the current relationship partner. In order to help clients get in touch with their transference issues, ask: "How is your spouse like one or both of your parents?" Follow this question with an opportunity to mobilize anger toward the parent that has been repressed in the muscles of the body. When a couple deals with the original focus of their anger, many relationship problems disappear or become less inflammatory.

The way in which couples make decisions is also stressed by core energetic therapists, because tension occurs when differences in problem-solving strategies become apparent. One person may respond emotionally, making decisions on the basis of strong feelings, whereas their partner may rule out emotion, trusting only reason and the facts and data upon which a rational answer is based. Others might exercise their will, at the expense of reason and emotion, saying: "this is the way I want it to be, so I will make it happen." If couples are to make solid, trustworthy decisions together, a balance between reason, will, and emotion is desirable. Short of that, it is important that partners, at least, become familiar with modes of behaving other than their habitual ones.

Sexuality is another area of life that core energetic therapists emphasize with couples. John Pierrakos teaches that every aspect of both people come into play in the couple's sexual life, including early developmental history, physical health, beliefs, images, religious and spiritual values, emotions, and cultural background (Wilner, 1998). When evaluating sexual relationships, the core energetic pyramid, with layers titled "body," "emotion," "mind," "will," and "spirit," makes an excellent diagnostic tool. The therapist first asks about physical problems and whether the clients can experience sensations in their bodies. To explore the connection and the unity between head, heart, and pelvis, clients are placed in the bow position which allows the therapist to determine how these parts are aligned and the number and types of splits between them. A question to ask couples is: "Where in your bodies do you stop the pleasure?"

The second level of the pyramid involves emotions and feelings. Many people are unaware of sexual feelings and are in denial about feelings concerning sex with their partners. For example, a middle-aged woman whose husband no longer approached her sexually needed the opportunity to explore her feelings of anger and rejection with him. Couples should be helped to share feelings about their own sexuality, their partner's sexuality, and their bodies. On the third level of the pyramid, the cognitive level, couples are asked to explore myths, stereotypes, attitudes, images, cognitions, and belief systems which affect their sex lives and play a role in their sexual response patterns. Attitudes and beliefs can enhance or inhibit sexual desire. For example, one study found that women who expected to have problems with menopause prior to entering menopause had more problems and less sex than women who did not expect to have problems (Cutler, 1991).

The fourth layer of the pyramid, the will, can also help or hinder sex. On the positive side, it helps people engage in a pleasurable, fulfilling physical relationship with a life partner, and, on the negative side, it leads some to engage in sexual behaviors which have nothing to do with love, such as manipulation, control, intimidation, and competition. The fifth level of the pyramid requires that couples open themselves to spiritual guidance during sex and focus on meditation, opening the heart, and exchanging energy from the chakras. Sexual energy, when it flows, helps to heal the splits within an individual and between the two partners. It may be used to unite the masculine and the feminine, the receptive and the assertive, and the physical and the spiritual aspects of their beings. Merging with a partner in lovemaking provides spiritual healing which balances the mundane tasks of daily living. In addition, sexual streamings, particularly when joined with love, resolve energetic problems and blockages, which if left alone may lead to illness and dysfunctional behavior. The movement of energy between the pelvis and the heart creates union, rejuvenation, and healing. Core energetics teaches couples to love their bodies in order to resolve sexual tensions and self-esteem issues. Reduction of symptoms follows from love of self, the surrender of control by the mind, and spontaneous experience of contact, touch, and meditation.

Techniques to help couples explore their sexuality include exercises to unify the head, heart, and pelvis, such as the bow, staccato breathing, and work with the roller, a core energetic tool that helps the person stretch, breathe, and ground. Some techniques join movement of the pelvis with movement in the jaw, body segments which hold sexual tension as well as anger. Sexual material left over from the family of origin is also explored, using structured role-plays and energetic work to bring forth honest responses to shame, rejection, and/or molestation by family members. These experiences are often followed by an intense release of feeling which may have interfered with the ability to experience sexual pleasure in the current relationship. Couples are also taught to work with the lower self in reference to sex. They may express their hidden, sexual cruelty toward each other. The expression of the negative truth in safe, cathartic exercises leads to the revelation of the higher sexual self and a fusion on the soul level of the two people.

Individuation versus fusion is another theme that occurs in couples therapy. Some people desire a lot of personal space, distance, and freedom in a relationship and feel suffocated if it does not exist. Others respond to personal space negatively, believing that its existence indicates a lack of closeness and affection. Core energetic theory calls for a merging of masculine and feminine energies and an experience of oneness and unity within a couple, at the level of the higher self. However, there are several conditions that must be met first. Union is not the same as fusion; two individuals may come together and unite without experiencing a loss of selfhood. Neither person submits to the other or sacrifices his or her own dreams and goals. For true union, there cannot be any control or manipulation. On the other hand, unification requires closeness and surrender. Feelings, experiences, and creative forces from the deepest level of one's being must be shared with the partner or lover. Core energetics stresses wholeness and unification for the couple without loss of individuation.

It is an extremely rewarding experience to work with couples using the theory, diagnostic methods, and energetic techniques offered by a core energetic approach. When relationships work well, each person who is involved is whole within himself or herself. Core energetics emphasizes unification for the individual and connection without loss of selfhood for the couple. This focus on integration, unification, and individuation, in which equal emphasis is placed on the body, emotions, mind, will, and spirit, enables true healing to occur for couples.

REFERENCES

Beck, A.T., & Freeman, A. (1990). *Cognitive therapy and personality disorders.* New York: The Guilford Press.

Broch, E. (1960). Compulsion to recreate and overcome childhood hurts. *Pathwork Lecture Series.* Box 66, Rt. 1, Madison, VA 22727: Seven Oaks Pathwork Center.

Cutler, W.B., & Garcia, C.R. (1992). *Menopause: A guide for women and the men who love them, revised edition.* New York: W. W. Norton & Co.

Glick, I.D., Clarkin, J.F., & Kessler, D.R. (1987). *Marital and family therapy.* New York: Grune & Stratton, Inc.

Lowen, A. (1971). *The language of the body.* New York: Collier Books (Original work published 1958).

Minuchin, S. & Fishman, H.C. (1981). *Family therapy techniques.* Cambridge, MA: Harvard University Press.

Pierrakos, J.C. (1986, October). *The history of core energetics.* Unpublished paper presented at a meeting of Core Energetic therapists, New York.

Pierrakos, J.C. (1990). *Core energetics: Developing the capacity to love and heal.* Mendocino, CA: LifeRhythm.

Pierrakos, J.C. (1997). *Eros, love & sexuality: The forces that unify man and woman.* Mendocino, CA: LifeRhythm.

Reich, W. (1972). *Character analysis* (3rd ed., V.R. Carfagno, Trans.). New York: Farrar, Straus, and Giroux (Original work published 1945).

Wilner, K.B. (in press). A core energetic approach to midlife sexuality. *Energy and consciousness.* New York: International Institute of Core Energetics.

Zuk, G.H., & Boszormenyi-Nagy, I. (1969). *Family therapy and disturbed families.* Palo Alto, CA: Science and Behavior Books.

Sexuality and Intimacy in Couples Therapy: The Journey of the Soul

Jacqueline A. Carleton

SUMMARY. In ages past, spiritual seekers left their close relationships for the seclusion of a monastery or a solitary journey, facing their dragons essentially alone. Today, however, many of us face the dragons within us as we undertake the tasks of differentiation and individuation. Thus, our relationships, if we allow them, can become the loci of our deepest self-exploration, leading to deepening intimacy with our partners. *[Article copies available for a fee from The Haworth Document Delivery Service: 1-800-342-9678. E-mail address: <getinfo@haworthpressinc.com> Website: <http://www.HaworthPress.com> © 2001 by The Haworth Press, Inc. All rights reserved.]*

KEYWORDS. Sexuality, intimacy, soul, journey, differentiation, individuation

There is nothing particularly new about the process of therapy. In some form or other, it exists in most known cultures. Human beings have always been concerned about the nature of the universe and their place in it. They have consulted myths, legends, oracles, priests, and shamans. All of us, in our

---

Jacqueline A. Carleton, PhD, is a senior faculty member of the International Institute of Core Energetics, Editor-in-Chief of *Energy and Consciousness*, The International Journal of Core Energetics, and a member of the Board of Directors of the United States Association of Body Psychotherapists.

Address correspondence to: Jacqueline A. Carleton, 115 East 92nd Street, Apt. 2A, New York, NY 10128 (E-mail: jacarleton@aol.com).

[Haworth co-indexing entry note]: "Sexuality and Intimacy in Couples Therapy: The Journey of the Soul." Carleton, Jacqueline A. Co-published simultaneously in *Journal of Couples Therapy* (The Haworth Press, Inc.) Vol. 10, No. 2, 2001, pp. 35-42; and: *Couples and Body Therapy* (ed: Barbara Jo Brothers) The Haworth Press, Inc., 2001, pp. 35-42. Single or multiple copies of this article are available for a fee from The Haworth Document Delivery Service [1-800-342-9678, 9:00 a.m. - 5:00 p.m. (EST). E-mail address: getinfo@haworthpressinc.com].

lives, are on heroic journeys, like those of Odysseus, Psyche, Don Quixote, or Dante's lone sojourner. We all at times tilt at windmills, pass apprehensively between Scylla and Charybdis, and explore the levels of our own private infernos. Who has not experienced emotional catharsis through fiction, poetry, music, theater, dance, or movement? Any effective therapy simply focusses these age-old human proclivities and illuminates with its intense light the path to health and wholeness in each therapeutic hour.

A few years ago, I began to come out of a five-year period in my life that I have since labeled "the dark night of my soul," in which, driven by life experiences and helped by therapy, my whole being underwent enormous changes. As I healed, I found myself in a relationship exponentially deeper on every level than I had ever experienced before. It took me to heights and, of course, to depths of myself that I had never known. More couples began to come into my practice for deep emotional and spiritual work. And simultaneously, it just "happened" that I was asked to teach more and more about love and sexuality. As usual, my own life, my clients' lives and my teaching all interacted with and reinforced each other.

For a long time, the journey of Ulysses/Odysseus had seemed to me the prototypical hero's journey. But, in the last few years, the myth of Eros and Psyche, written a few centuries later, has seemed even better to illustrate the essence of the conscious journey. In it, Psyche (Soul) has lived an unconscious life, too beautiful even to be wed, but worshipped from afar by such multitudes that she excites the jealousy of the goddess Aphrodite. Finally left on a mountaintop by her family to await a marriage with death, she is whisked away by an unknown rescuer to a paradise-like environment. Love comes to her in paradise, only in the night under cover of darkness, just as escaping from difficult, terrifying, or torturous times to the relief of paradise, we are often content to ask no questions for a time. But then our souls become restless for expansion and we begin to question again. In the myth, the questions are spoken by Psyche's sisters, and she acts on their counsel to hold up the light to the eros she has enjoyed under cover of darkness. When she does, her world turns upside down: Love flees, and she is catapulted out of paradise as she tries to cling to his heel.

Thus the real quest begins: the journey (back) to love. Eros is the awakener, the tasks of individual development remain. Psyche confronts the questions we must ask ourselves and our clients: What is our life task, what is our life plan, for what are we here on earth? What inner and outer marriage do we seek? As Psyche confronts the tasks set for her by Aphrodite to regain Eros, we see how love can be the torturer and purifier of the soul, leading to growth, individuation, and the marriage of our masculine and feminine aspects.

In ages past, seekers of the deeper mysteries of life left their homes and close relationships for the seclusion of a monastery or a solitary journey, facing their dragons with only their faith for companionship. For many people today, however, the wilderness that brings us face to face with our gods and demons is in our intimate relationships. In our personal work, we confront our lower selves, our shadows, as did Ann and Tom described below. But, in their relationship, they, like Psyche in the myth, were challenged to illuminate the interaction between their own dark sides and those of their partner. Perhaps only in our century have people sought to unite, in themselves and in their relationships, the three forces of love, sexuality, and eros. Only our hearts and bodies can initially select our mates, for without the deep bonds of love expressed through our bodies, it is difficult if not impossible to enjoy rather than merely accept or tolerate the mirror our relationships become for us. However, in an article entitled "The Forces of Love, Sex, and Eros" (Pierrakos, 1987), John Pierrakos suggests that, while eros may initially provide a very strong attraction between two people, the growth of deep love must be a conscious choice on the part of both partners. So, the only way for love and sexual attraction to flourish in a long term relationship is for both partners to continually reveal new depths in themselves to the other.

Jungian psychologists would refer to this heroic soul journey as the process of individuation or differentiation. This process is absolutely vital to the health of intimate, and especially sexual, relationships. According to David Schnarch, to whom I am deeply indebted for many of the ideas in this article:

> Differentiation is a basic life force that propels every living thing to grow and become distinctly itself while remaining part of its species' social unit. In humans it shows up as the ability to maintain a clearly defined sense of yourself in close proximity to significant others, especially when pressured to conform. It involves the ability to self-soothe your own anxiety, and resilience to others' anxiety, which permits responses determined by clear thinking and modulated feelings rather than emotional reactivity. These are necessary characteristics if sexual novelty and intimacy are to flourish in long-term relationships. (1991, p. 120)

In order to know deeply and be known, we must be willing to become mature, differentiated human beings capable of expressing who we really are even when our partner does *not* respond with affirmation, empathy, or approval. Because our relationships mean so much to us, we collude with each other rather than risk severely disrupting or losing them. Many therapists also collude with this collusion. An example of such collusion would be a spoken or unspoken agreement that if I reveal something about myself, then you must reveal something about yourself. Or, if I reveal something of which I feel, for example, ashamed or guilty, you have to comfort or approve of me, at least for sharing it with you. Therapists often coach couples to make such agreements (Schnarch, 1991, p. 142).

Probably the deepest, most primordial fear we bring to relationship is our fear of what is inside ourselves. As we draw closer to one another, many of these inner fears can be articulated. Many people are afraid of losing their power, their very selves, in relationships. For them, it is a challenge to balance listening to their inner voice and listening to their partner. Others are afraid of being abandoned by their partner and have to learn how not to abandon themselves. Those who fear commitment often have difficulty maintaining their boundaries and must learn to say "no" if they are chronic rescuers or caretakers.

Ann, a high-ranking communications executive, came to me with her husband, Tom, an affable lawyer, for help with their difficulties with their children, and for the growing distance in their sexual relationship. In their fifth session, as we began to ground and center in preparation for intense emotional work, Ann spontaneously began to cry, softly at first, then harder as I began to massage her neck and shoulders. Tom stood by, looking baffled and helpless.

Ann: "Why am I always responsible for Katie and Laurie's behavior? You never impose any limits! When we go to a restaurant, you don't care what they do! I always have to see that they are polite and try to keep them entertained and in their seats so they don't trip the waitress."

Tom: "Ann, you're just overreacting as usual. The girls are fine; nobody cares if they get up and walk around a little. Why are you so uptight?"

At this juncture, I asked Ann if she would like to express her resentment physically, by hitting a pile of pillows I keep in my office with a soft bat or tennis racket. She chose the tennis racket. I asked Tom if he felt centered enough to stand behind the pillows so Ann could express her frustration directly to him. He grounded himself and agreed, saying he felt pretty frustrated, too. I handed him a racket as well. Instructing them to hit down and make a sound at first and then say whatever came into their minds as they hit, I grabbed and held the stack of pillows firmly.

"You're controlling," "You're a wuss," the insults flew back and forth for a moment until I stopped them and told them to speak their feelings, not their judgments. As they resumed hitting the pillows, feelings began to emerge, "I'm angry," "I'm hurt," "I feel useless," "I feel abandoned."

Ann began to cry again, softly and deeply now, without the angry tone her voice had held at first. She said to Tom that she had married him because he was so unlike her father, seeming so kind and caring, but somehow his failure to discipline their children left her feeling tense and abandoned. They both looked puzzled.

After a brief silence, Ann began to speak of how trapped she felt as a child by her father's baffling and brutal physical punishments. If he loved her, which he clearly did, how could he strike her with such violence in response to minor infractions? Suddenly, she fell to her knees in front of the pile of pillows, hugging them and at the same time pummeling them with her fists. Her sobs deepened. She began to cough and choke. This continued until she found her voice to say, "No! No! No!" as she hit. Her rage built as she pummeled the pillows. Then, as she grew tired, her sobbing softened slowly and subsided, finally, into gentle weeping. As she shed the last few tears, her face shone with a realization: "I never understood until now how his blows hurt me *inside*." Released from his role as the "bad guy," Tom moved over to her, squatted down and touched her hand tentatively. Without looking up, she reached out and grabbed his forearm. Taking that as a signal to comfort her, he wrapped first his arms and then his whole body around her, taking her in his lap as she continued to alternate between sobs and gentle weeping.

From that realization, we were able to go on to discover how trapped she felt by the actually quite acceptable behavior of her 2- and 5-year-olds who seemed to her so like the unruly younger siblings for whom she had always been responsible and for whose misbehavior her parents always held her accountable. Her body had held the key to the relationship between her difficulties at work, her early family situation, and her present love life. Although she had discussed it many times in previous couples therapy, she had never before made a visceral, emotional connection between her present feelings and her father's sudden and arbitrary punishments.

But, it still remained to bring it to her present relationship with Tom. She began to realize how she kept him at arm's length with her tension about the children. By trying to control both him and them as she had felt controlled, she was not allowing him to be fully himself, and Tom, for his own reasons, found it easier to collude passively with her control rather than risk showing her who he truly was. This left Ann bored and Tom resentful but secretly pleased with himself. In an atmosphere like this, there was certainly little room for sexual intimacy. Ann withdrew, denying herself sex. Tom masturbated resentfully by himself. In order to experience full sexuality they would have to challenge their fear of intimacy directly.

Not until she was able to "fight back" and say "no" could Ann's body-mind allow her to feel and act differently. This is what core energetic therapy (Pierrakos, 1987) emphasizes: finding the connection to the core of one's self, the pathway leading to the love and pleasure that is every being's birthright. Not until Ann could feel how her inner being had been damaged and how she herself continued her hitherto unconscious self-punishment could she begin to heal the inner wound, take control of that aspect of her life, forgive both her father and herself, and really begin an adult sexual relationship with her husband.

Many people tend to stifle uncomfortable feelings and end up repeating painful patterns until they feel completely stuck. By focussing on the discovery of how the life force can be blocked in their bodies and how thought processes, belief systems, and images are imprisoned within these blocks, couples can, through breathing, expressive work, physical movement, and conscious intention, release these blocks, connect more deeply to their core selves, and feel more vitally and passionately alive.

Couples come to therapy with different needs and goals. Some have repressed a substantial part of their feelings; others are flooded by them. No two people are alike and each requires a different combination of support, confrontation, body work, imagery, analysis of dreams, artwork or music, empathic listening, and explanation.

To aid in finding how we identify with our own distortions, how we cling to false beliefs, and how we are afraid to surrender to the joy that life can bring, I often employ the concepts of the "higher self," "lower self," and "mask self." Sometimes it helps to have clients sit on three separate chairs as they explore the interactions of each of these different aspects of the self in their relationships. The higher self or core or soul is who we really are at our best, in truth and in joy and in love. As we go through life, this precious center of our being, in response to pain, often becomes armored by the defensive emotions of anger, rage, fear, spite, terror, and destructiveness; and who we really are is hidden. These defensive emotions we refer to as the lower self because we judge them to be unworthy of us and yet we at least dimly know they are there. So, in order to abrogate their power, we cover them with a mask self which is more acceptable to others and to ourselves. The mask covers "compromise" emotions, such as jealousy, envy, guilt, hostility, pride, blame, self-pity, justification, and rationalization. Our mask is our socially acceptable self, what Reich called the "character."

By expressing physically and verbally each of these aspects, couples can begin to untangle some of the cords that bind them to old patterns. Thus, a mask of serenity may cover jealousy and greed. If a person can find and express the jealousy and greed, he or she will be led back to the pain and deprivation that surely underlie them. And, if these primary emotions can find expression, the couples' organism's emotional self-regenerating system will be activated and their true generosity, a quality of their core, will emerge and help to heal the original deprivation as they give to each other in the present. Ann had been stuck in her mask of responsible politeness with her children and with her husband at home. As she learned to express her lower self-emotions of rage and pain in the therapy and as she found increased energy in them, her higher self of love and compassion was able to emerge. Inspired by her, Tom was also able to mobilize his hitherto hidden aggression and become less passive with her and with the children. He was able to approach her sexually rather than retreating to masturbate alone. This was only the beginning of their path toward differentiation and deeper sexuality and intimacy in their relationship.

Judith Saly, in the introduction to her book, *The Pathwork of Relationship* has said that "if life is a school, relationship is its university" (Saly, 1993, p. xiii). For it is in intimate relationships that our growth is most challenged and perhaps is where, as Wilhelm Reich (1942) categorically insists in *Function of the Orgasm*, our emotional health can be partly defined: "My contention is that every individual who has managed to preserve a bit of naturalness knows that there is only one thing wrong with neurotic patients: the lack of full and repeated sexual satisfaction . . . " (p. 85), which he defines as "the capacity for ultimate vegetatively involuntary surrender . . . Orgiastic potency is the biological primal and basic function which man has in common with all living organisms. . . . This occurs frequently in individuals who are able to concentrate tender as well as their sensual feelings on a partner."

Following Reich, most schools of sex therapy, certainly from Masters and Johnson to Helen Singer Kaplan, are based on the "sex is a natural function" model (Schnarch, 1987). As far as it goes, it is absolutely correct. But there is much more, for as is being increasingly documented today, our biological responses are mediated by, and more correctly, interactive with, our thoughts, feelings and perceptions.

Intimate sex is utterly terrifying and mysterious, but it is also a spiritual path. If we crave the ecstasy, we must be prepared to undergo the agony of it. What is that agony? Exposure, helplessness and inevitable eventual loss. But, if we are willing to know deeply and be deeply known by our partner, it is possible to have a sexual relationship far beyond the limits of what most people or sex therapists would ever hope to experience (Schnarch, 1991, p. 142).

It takes tremendous courage, integrity, and faith to *risk* intimacy. Odysseus and Psyche were engaged in endeavors leading them toward their beloveds, but it is significant that on that journey, each traveled alone, often in despair. I would suggest that we of the 20th century travel this path both together and alone. Although I feel the journey is richer and ultimately more challenging shared with a beloved as inspiration and irritant along the way, there is a sense in which the *work* of the quest is essentially alone.

If we allow our true selves to enter them, our relationships can become an ideal environment for the nourishment of each of us. When you choose to relate to another, you are choosing to be affected. We often have the fantasy that the other should change, not ourselves.

But, our character will be ground and polished through the actions and character of our loved ones, through the praise, criticism, frustration, excitement, actions, and inactions of those persons. To know that relationship has a purpose is to be willing to bear the challenges that lie along its path. But it is also to rejoice and be glad, to be exuberant and playful, to bask in the companionship of the person who delights us. As our relationships and our shared lives and work become increasingly intertwined, we must strive harder and use ever-deeper resources of courage to be true to ourselves. But, at the same time, we must use those same resources to reveal ever deeper parts of ourselves to the other, for only by so doing will our relationships continue to grow, deepen, and enrich themselves.

To summarize, deep intimacy in a committed relationship does not come naturally; it is a learned ability and an acquired taste (Schnarch, 1991). As we develop, grow, and, yes, age, we will become more differentiated as individuals and better able to validate ourselves. We will be able, in the crucible of a committed relationship, to look at our human capacities for hatred, sadism, control, our secret needs and insecurities, our sexual fantasies, and our terrors of rejection and of being ultimately alone. By facing these aspects of ourselves and each other, by giving up the remaining vestiges of the child's hopes for unconditional love, we will truly find each other. The paradox is that acute awareness of our ultimate loneliness and separateness will lead us to greater intimacy than we could ever have dreamed of. Rather than fusion, real intimacy consists in deeply knowing oneself in the presence of the other while recognizing the other's immutable separateness. Only in complete surrender to our core self and its immutable singularity will we find ultimate union with each other.

It takes tremendous courage, integrity and faith to risk such a journey. But, at its apogee is self-transcendence, true spirituality, and fun.

REFERENCES

Pierrakos, J. (1987). *Core energetics, developing the capacity to love and heal.* Mendocino, CA: LifeRhythm Publications.

Reich, W. (1942). *The function of orgasm.* New York: Farrar, Strauss.

Saly, J. & Pierrakos, E. (1993). *Creating union, the pathwork of relationship.* Madison, VA: Pathwork Press.

Schnarch, David M. (1991). *Constructing the sexual crucible, an integration of sexual and marital therapy.* New York: W.W. Norton.

Schnarch, D. (1997). *Passionate marriage.* New York: W.W. Norton.

Keeping It Up

Marcel A. Duclos

SUMMARY. Clients benefit from an eclectic approach. In the case of a presenting problem such as failure to maintain an erection, the assistance of body psychotherapy in the form of Core Energetics brings additional dimensions to couples work. In this case, only the male partner came to the office; but both benefited from the integration of bodywork into the therapeutic enterprise. The client needed access to his body to incorporate the insights and the skills of other therapeutic work. This article offers a sample of the work. *[Article copies available for a fee from The Haworth Document Delivery Service: 1-800-342-9678. E-mail address: <getinfo@haworthpressinc.com> Website: <http://www.HaworthPress. com> © 2001 by The Haworth Press, Inc. All rights reserved.]*

KEYWORDS. Body psychotherapy, bodywork, Core Energetics

For a man, keeping it up when you want to or when your partner wants you to presents both a risk and an opportunity. For Robert, keeping it up on demand or on desire confronted him with a risk. Would he embarrass himself again? Would he lose his breath? Would he recoil to his side of the bed in a

---

Marcel A. Duclos, MTh, MEd, LACD, LCPC, LCS, CCMHC, is Professor Emeritus, Jungian Psychotherapist, Developmental Psychologist and a practicing theologian and philosopher. He currently serves as a consultant/therapist/family specialist in Child Protective Services for the New Hampshire Division of Child, Youth and Family Services. Honored as an educator, human services pioneer and outstanding contributor to the field of Substance Abuse Counseling, Marcel A. Duclos has added the practical wisdom of Core Energetics Body Psychotherapy to his current practice as a psychotherapist/clinical supervisor. He serves as Chair of the Training Standards Committee for the United States Association of Body Psychotherapy.

[Haworth co-indexing entry note]: "Keeping It Up." Duclos, Marcel A. Co-published simultaneously in *Journal of Couples Therapy* (The Haworth Press, Inc.) Vol. 10, No. 2, 2001, pp. 43-47; and: *Couples and Body Therapy* (ed: Barbara Jo Brothers) The Haworth Press, Inc., 2001, pp. 43-47. Single or multiple copies of this article are available for a fee from The Haworth Document Delivery Service [1-800-342-9678, 9:00 a.m. - 5:00 p.m. (EST). E-mail address: getinfo@haworthpressinc.com].

near fetal position? Would he once again revisit the feelings of shame he experienced as a boy when his mother inserted the routine suppositories? Would he want the consolation of a few beers to distract him from the memory of his mother belittling his childhood erection? How could he face his partner in the morning? She had turned away in disappointment and disgust. He did not know how to stand up for himself in the relationship. While he revealed his story, I thought of him as a performer dreaming of the night's theater but fearing the curtain call. He came to therapy with a diagnosable case of stage fright.

The urologist and the psychiatrist had both ruled out any anatomical, physiological, biochemical, and neurological etiology to his erectile problem. All efforts in the previous six months of cognitive-behavioral sex therapy had not ameliorated the situation. He did not suffer from any major mental disorder. He had gained knowledge. He had not been able to put it into practice. The partners were at an impasse. She did not want to join him in therapy. It was his problem to fix. She had enough of her problems to deal with in her own therapy given her strain and trauma-filled childhood. That is how he came to call for an appointment upon the recommendation of the psychiatrist/ sex-therapist. "Can you help me?" he asked. "Come for a consultation," I replied after the brief statement of the presenting problem. That was it. He wanted to come. We could consult. I would assess. We would decide on the work.

Robert stands five feet eight inches and weighs about one-hundred-and-eighty pounds. He is muscular with the shoulders, chest, buttocks, and legs of an athlete. He shook my hand without determination and put on an I'm-a-nice-fellow smile as I welcomed him into the office. His small head and soft young facial features did not fit his body. He was successful at his sales job where he combined his love of mathematics with human relations. He knew how to please and placate. I remember the temptation to challenge his passive dependent style right then in the first session: a clue to how he invited the replication of earlier demeaning exchanges in his family of origin.

His father, who had always been an absent figure in Robert's life, had recently died after a brief illness. Robert grieved the loss of ever being able to have a father-son relationship full of pride for a job well done. "I had never measured up," he said. In fact, Robert's two older brothers had found countless ways to put him down and humiliate him. They made fun of his smaller penis as a younger boy. They submitted him to unexpected "wedgies." The random schedule of abuse left him anxious, apprehensive, and avoidant. They treated him like a beaten down dog. He could not stand up to them. He had no voice in the house. Once in his teen years, his mother hardly had any time for him. He learned to be alone and to act as if he needed no one. He did not date until he went to college and then only under the influence of alcohol.

Until this relationship, he had never engaged in sex unless he was intoxicated. As he put it, "I have no experience because I was always drunk." He had been both sober and celibate for the last five years. An early failure to keep it up during his early recovery had settled in as performance anxiety: stage fright! Robert had just celebrated his thirty-fifth birthday. I experienced him more like an unsure teenager than a grown man. This would require something other than the repair of an erector set because it was not broken. It was energetically cut off. I accepted working with him, to do couples therapy with a physically absent partner.

We are coming up to our second year anniversary. Robert has not always liked the body psychotherapy. Once he understood what it was that he brought to the interpersonal relationship with his fiancée (yes, they were engaged after the first year), he consciously and courageously confronted himself not only in the therapy sessions, but also in anxious moments with her. He literally had to grow up. With his father transference toward me finally emerging into a valuing of himself as an adult male, he was able to withdraw his mother transference from his fiancée and thereby reduce his paralyzing fear of rejection and humiliation. He left a secure job during this time to take on more administrative duties. He sold his house, and they bought one together. He made decisions for himself in spite of her anxious objections. He learned how to make relatively permanent changes in his old behavior patterns in small incremental steps without first adjusting to her emotional reactions like a chameleon. He ultimately dared to take charge of their lovemaking scene now and again instead of gearing up for sexual jousting.

What was the glue to the work that included Jungian dream analysis, structural, strategic, and systems family therapy guided interactions that involved some limited gestalt role-play and occasional psychodrama? It was the insertion of energy and consciousness into moments of bodywork as we moved progressively into body psychotherapy.

Robert stood feet close together and toes pointed out while he put more weight on his right side, which was slightly forward. His shoulders rose to his ears as his head and neck sank into his upper chest. His head and chin jutted forward out of alignment with his spine. His shallow breath allowed a slightly labored exhalation. He received occasional treatment for asthma; otherwise he reported no other ailment. His eyes, at first, joined his mouth in projecting an outward welcome; but then his facial muscles shifted to a display of apprehensive retreat. Whereas his chest was thick and muscular, his shoulders folded forward and down. His upper chest was visibly concave beneath his shirt. His pelvis tipped forward; his buttocks tight and out. He presented with that familiar military pulled-in abdomen posture. A slight paunch rested on his belt. Nothing moved from his diaphragm to his ankles. Although his legs were in proportion to his torso in size and muscle mass, his knees were locked however he changed his stances. Standing in his stocking feet, one could not miss observing the relatively small 7 1/2-shoe size. In that position, a lightweight could have easily knocked him on his back with one quick push. His body had taken on the structure and shape of a push over. He was a "pushover."

Robert lived in his head in anticipation of outer threats. Whatever he could not deflect with his charm, he would defend against with his bulk. Yet, he was a pushover since he did not live in his lower half. He was not present nor was he conscious of any movement because of his inflexible posture. How could the structural mechanics of his sexual apparatus obey the signal systems of desire and stimulation when frozen at the very cellular level? He still could not move of his own accord, armed as he was with the insights and strategies of various therapeutic interventions. Neither could she move him to a sustainable erection because of the old memories and defenses remembered, to be specific, in his member–physically and symbolically. So we set about to make connections, to rewire his body. How else would he be able to execute his intent to show his love, to make love to the women who would still marry him?

Learning, as mentioned above, is a relatively permanent change in behavior that is maintained through practice. We were now facing the down and dirty part of our contract: putting all the pieces together. We practiced how to stand. He aligned his feet. He unlocked his knees. He leveled his pelvis, brought his pubis forward, relaxed his buttocks, anus, and entire perineum. We practiced bending over and letting his head, hands, arms, torso hang over while breathing deeply. He felt the solidity of his lower body holding him steady: knees slightly bent, each foot planted like a tripod, large muscles vibrating to the flow of energy, and consciousness vivifying his stance. He confronted his fear of letting his head hang loose, of not being able to control the moment with his eyes, of being in a vulnerable position. We found the muscular holding in his shoulders and neck. In between the intermittent cascading bows, he willfully brought his awareness to those deadened masses of tissue being probed, softened, and warmed by the healing hands of the guide/therapist. One day, he reported having found himself being right there in the moment, like a click, when he took his grounding stance in a confrontation with a coworker. Like someone who finally, after much dedication, hits that note, mixes that color, reaches that peak, Robert said he now had hope that he would be able to successfully inhabit his body more and more often at will in the future. He was touching his solar plexus while he spoke.

He was encouraged to move on. Together we challenged his fear of exposure in the back bend: feet planted, knees bent, pelvis relaxed as in the bow. In that position, his throat, his rib cage, his heart, his center all lay open and unprotected. How to stay firmly planted, feel the rising panic and not run away in an emotional collapse? Robert fixed his eyes straight ahead and reached up and back with his arms. He consciously confronted the spasms between his sternum and his navel as well as his halting breath. His face reddened. He coughed. He trembled. This was a more difficult task that required a step-by-step approach. We returned to the physical expression of anger by hitting pillows from a grounded stance. He put his pelvis into it. He learned to add words to an aggressive bite and jaw. He lay on the couch and slammed his legs and arms at first in a deliberately cautious manner and then with the intensity of a blue-faced toddler who could swear like a trooper. Memories returned and negative self-beliefs found voice for the first time. He agreed to do EMDR to metabolize this lingering tyranny and to install more accurate positive self-statements. He surprised himself when he could visualize the scene: standing up for himself without recoil or advance in an exchange with his fiancée which in the past had undermined any hope of self-soothing. He had tasted his emerging differentiation.

So we proceeded further with body psychotherapy. Robert agreed to combine work on the roller to continue the work of connecting his longing for love and his desire for sex. He wanted to give a fuller expression of his affection. He wanted to express that affection sexually. Arching backward on the twenty-inch cloth-covered hard wood roller, he completed the additional breakthroughs. He learned to breathe further down into his abdomen, to sense the difference between a constricted genital area and a sensory relaxed one. He invited and accepted the manipulation of his jaw, neck, chest, mid-section and abdomen. He screamed in fear. He cried in anguish. He suffered spasms in resistance to the movement of energy and in release of the same. He learned how to consciously honor his choice to love, his yearning for eros and his urge for sex.

Robert and his fiancée married at the end of our time together. He discovered that she was not so threatening in her demand for great sexual performances. She rejoiced at his increased staying power in and out of bed. He was surprised that her anxiety in other matters lessened because he took charge more often, and made his moves when the scene felt erotic to him and called for a leading man.

Nothing is perfect; nothing is complete in this world. Freud told us a long time ago that at best we dispel the darkness of ignorance, we bring the neuroses to the light of consciousness. Character, to use an old word in the Reichian tradition, remains for life. We all experience, given enough age, the lingering and reappearing of our earliest personality traits. Robert is still burdened by unsatisfied needs; but he has discovered that his body offers him the gifts of companionship, of conversation, of truth. He now has a partner-body. In the Jungian tradition, one would say that Robert enjoys a greater measure of union of what were, in the past, opposites.

When we parted, both Robert and I could realistically celebrate his keeping it up.

Couples Therapy as a Formative Process

Stanley Keleman
Sylvia Adler

SUMMARY. Becoming a couple means that two bodies come together to form a bond. In forming this bond, the partners' bodies use innate or learned patterns–how to be aroused, how to be tender or kind, how to reach out. These body postures can grow and mature over the lifetime of the relationship, or not. Couples seek professional help when they cannot end the shapes of bonding that no longer serve them and organize the next shapes of adult relating. This article presents the formative model of couples therapy, a somatically based experiential approach that emphasizes how partners use themselves bodily in their relationship and how they can reorganize their patterns bodily to grow both themselves and their relationship. A case example is given. *[Article copies available for a fee from The Haworth Document Delivery Service: 1-800-342-9678. E-mail address: <getinfo@ haworthpressinc.com> Website: <http://www.HaworthPress.com> © 2001 by The Haworth Press, Inc. All rights reserved.]*

Stanley Keleman has been practicing and developing Formative Psychology and its applications in somatic psychotherapy and personal growth work for over 30 years. He is a pioneer in his study of the body and of the ways in which the body forms relationships to itself and others. Through his writings and practice, he has developed a methodology and conceptual framework for the life of the body. His publications include *Emotional Anatomy, Love: A Somatic View, Patterns of Distress, Bonding,* and most recently, *Myth and the Body.*

Sylvia Adler, LCSW, BCD, a cofounder of the Family Institute of Chicago, is a long-time practitioner and teacher of family and couples therapy. She has been professionally associated with Keleman's work for over 20 years and has published articles on the Family Body approach in the *Journal of Somatic Experience.*

Address correspondence to: Center for Energetic Studies, 2045 Francisco Street, Berkeley, CA 94709.

[Haworth co-indexing entry note]: "Couples Therapy as a Formative Process." Keleman, Stanley, and Sylvia Adler. Co-published simultaneously in *Journal of Couples Therapy* (The Haworth Press, Inc.) Vol. 10, No. 2, 2001, pp. 49-59; and: *Couples and Body Therapy* (ed: Barbara Jo Brothers) The Haworth Press, Inc., 2001, pp. 49-59. Single or multiple copies of this article are available for a fee from The Haworth Document Delivery Service [1-800-342-9678, 9:00 a.m. - 5:00 p.m. (EST). E-mail address: getinfo@haworthpressinc.com].

KEYWORDS. Somatic, formative therapy, somatic-emotional exercises, couples, cobodying, psychotherapy

Central to somatic thinking is this concept: How a person acts is more important than how he or she feels or thinks. With couples, this means: Do the partners have somatic abilities that enable them to act or grow to satisfy their own and their partner's needs? Do these abilities include ways to sustain contact or maintain a distance? Do they include ways to keep an open-ended system that is capable of ongoing growth and maturation? Feeling and thinking come from how the soma uses itself.

The way people act is grounded in their physical postures, gestures, and muscular attitudes. Together, these organismic states form somatic stances; mostly they are outside the awareness of most people. In couples therapy, we ask the partners to experience their physical attitudes and somatic stances. In a relationship, the ways that couples form intimacy or create distance are influenced by somatic stances.

In using formative therapy with couples, often the first task is to work with each partner separately and then with the partners together, so that they can begin to recognize these somatic stances in themselves. Once they have recognized these stances, they can learn to influence their intensity and pervasiveness. The more somatic stances a person has, the more distinct the somatic patterns are, and the more choices there are for behavior. The more choices there are, the more opportunities the person has to sustain contact or maintain distance. Continuing growth and maturation depend on the ability to form an ever-wider range of somatic-emotional expressions, and thereby to deepen relationships.

Generally, couples seek professional help when they cannot make a transition to the next stage of adult relating. This article presents a somatically based clinical model for helping couples. The work is experiential, emphasizing how partners use themselves bodily to form relationships. The goals are to teach couples to experience their styles of relating and to influence them, to experience the ways they use their bodies to come close or stay away, and to organize and manage the transition to different behavior. Formative therapy helps couples to learn to make transitions, to feel their bodies more, to relate to their present reality, and to understand the ambiguity of the future.

Unless couples have ways to influence their somatic patterns and the unspoken contracts between partners that come from these patterns, they will be unable to affect their relationship to an appreciable extent.

THE FORMATIVE PROCESS

Life is a process of forming. There is a continual reshaping of our bodily self, from the unformed infant to the formed adult. Either we live this forming unreflectively, or we volitionally participate in influencing our inherited responses.

The formative process is innate. Each time there is a new reforming, the process moves in stages. The first stage is an ending, the disassembling of an established form. This ending is actually a conceiving stage. Disorganization is accompanied by intense somatic-emotional excitement. This excitement catalyzes the possibility of new behavior. This intense period is followed by a second stage, a middle ground between what was and what is not yet. Middle ground is an unformed or porous state, a womb for new form. The last stage is one of stabilization, a form which emerges with a feeling of competence to perform and to contain new behavior.

Relationship is a pulsating pattern between two bodies that grows through these stages of ending, incubation, and emergence of new behavior. Intense energies are continually expanding, unforming, and forming us. These growth transitions are expansive and porous, rigid and dense. We experience our own and the other's expansion and contraction as closeness and distance.

Relationships are essential for personal growth. They provide a stable emotional atmosphere, a palpable somatic state that is inclusive and that promotes the growth of somatic-emotional complexity. Within adult relationships, we and the other have a felt sense of belonging, of being inside something bigger. When adults form a bond as a couple, they establish a primary somatic-emotional relationship that supports their continuing emotional intimacy and growth as individual adults. As growing adults, we participate in forming that relationship. An adult relationship is bigger than each individual; it is elastic and inclusive. We can take a distance without disassociating; we can enter deeply into the intimacy without being engulfed.

Body Proximity

Relationships have to do with body proximity–how two bodies form and regulate closeness and distance with each other. Bodies naturally want to come close together as well as to keep their distance. The body uses its cortex to negotiate how it will achieve this. The soma grows according to how it influences its emotional patterns of coming close and letting others come close.

The process of closeness and distance, and intimacy and separation, is pulsatory in nature. This pulse of closeness and distance has an inner organizing cycle. There is the beginning, intense phase–a swollen excitement. People who are falling in love have these expansive feelings. In the next phase, the porous stage, boundaries start to assemble to contain the excitement of attraction. The third organizing phase involves a firming of the assembled structure. The structure grows into a thickened, dense form that barely changes. This thickened form overprotects and excludes, creating a separation and distance from the other person. Fortunately, the cortex can influence these emotional pulses, both extending and curtailing them. This process is how we use ourselves to influence intimacy.

One example of the pulse of closeness and distance is the pattern of nonavailability and pursuit. This is organized by one partner's body pulling back or shrinking, ever so slightly, making that partner less available and allowing less of the outside world in. The other partner may either collapse or cling or stiffen to avoid feelings of rejection. Usually the distanced person will reach forward in pursuit of the withdrawer, either in anger or in desperation to avoid abandonment. This emotional pattern between two people of retreat and pursuit is also a somatic pattern of withdrawal and collapse.

In formative work, we call attention to these somatic-emotional patterns. People learn to recognize and influence these patterns, to disorganize and reassemble a different personal adult form of relating.

Individual Shapes

There are distinct individual body shapes. These are closely related to the stages of the formative process. For example, persons with porous shapes have some form but not enough. Persons with a porous shape are over-empathetic; they take on the other person's state, but may not have enough form to sustain with assertion their own somatic shape or need. In contrast, overstructured, dense persons are too conservative and reserved; trapped in their compressed inwardness, they tend not to extend or make themselves vulnerable. In a relationship, it is impossible for them to reach out or to empathize with someone else. At the same time, the ability of densely structured persons to be determined and loyal makes them feel powerful.

A person's individual shape has much to do with how he/she relates to other people. Dense, over-structured people fear being unformed or overwhelmed by excitation; they withdraw and push others away. They dominate with their stiffness, which gives feelings of pleasure or power. Porous, under-formed people have difficulty maintaining boundaries; they give in and yield their identity. They have a sense of power in their ambiguity.

Each somatic structure serves a function in a relationship. The swollen structure generates eruptions in himself or the other person. These eruptions can either break down a relationship or create a sense of excitement. The porous structure is receptive to the experiences of others, empathetic. The rigid structure makes relationship distinct and repeatable. Dense structures give relationships durability and reliability.

THE FORMATIVE STAGES OF COUPLES RELATIONSHIPS

There is a self-generating growth sequence in couple relationships. Each stage in this sequence has a distinct somatic emotional shape. Each phase of coupling generates the next phase, with its experiences of bonding and its problems. The growth of the relationship facilitates, stabilizes, and deepens somatic-emotional and cognitive experience and values.

This formative cycle is how we generate continuous growth and deepen or mature the soma and its relationships. Partners often do not know how to influence somatic structure to affect conflicts and problems of their own formative process. They do not know that the shape of a relationship grows and changes; they do not know how to end one shape and phase and reorganize the next. The person who says, "I feel tenderness toward my spouse, but the only way I can express it is by doing things for her," has a somatic problem—the problem of not being able to directly organize a physical proximity that is tender. Unless the individual is able to learn to use his body to express tenderness, he will be limited in his ability to deepen intimacy with his spouse.

Each stage of couple bonding can be experienced as a challenge to somatic growth or as a threat to be avoided. These stages in a couple's relationship can be either satisfying and supportive or met with dread.

Stage One.
One Inside the Other: The Umbilical-Uterine Bond

When couples initially bond, there is a somatic-emotional intensity. This swollen and intense excitement melts boundaries and engulfs; the other person is in us and/or we are in the other person. This sharing of an inside with another is the basis of empathy. It is a catalyst for the growth of a new relationship. However, if this kind of bond is perpetuated as in romanticism, it inhibits growth and individuality. While the function of the uterine bond is to incubate growth and form, it can become a relationship of power and dependency. If only one person in this relationship can act as an adult, the other person is kept small and unformed.

Stage Two.
One as Part of the Other: The Attached Bond

Porosity begins as the couple emerges from the excitatory storm. The partners remain attached, but individual form is growing. The partners need each other to support a fragile, unsteady organization of relating. There is a recognition of the two somatic selves, but in the sense of "your body completes me" or "my body, my ability to function, depends on your body." Both partners are reluctant to be separate and will try to prevent separations by clinging or being clung to. In the growth phase, the porous pattern lets people learn to "co-body" and coexist and to support each other's growing separateness. This stage facilitates the growth of the pulse pattern of closeness-separateness that is essential to all intimate relationships. However, if this pattern does not develop, there is either isolation or clinging.

Stage Three.
Separation and Extrusion of One by the Other

One way some couples form packages of separateness is to be emotionally explosive. Another way is to begin a gradual process of detachment, each one withdrawing bodily to exclude the other. Partners may dramatize differences in order to pursue separateness or stiffen against their rushes of wanting to be close. When the partners are able to form distinct bodies, then the pulse of separate-close can become the elastic relationship of two adults and deepen bodily closeness. The ability to influence the intensity of somatic-emotional closeness and separateness is the adult dynamic of intimacy. The dynamic is to share experience; then to be separate so each can form himself/herself in a personal way; and then again to share experience. This is growth and deepening that adds meaning and value to a relationship. However, couples who cannot transcend this stage of somatic-emotional separation may continue for years in a kind of alienation or surface cooperation. For many other couples, this stage becomes the prelude to divorce.

Stage Four.
Intimacy: The Relationship of Giving and Receiving

In organizing the pulse of closeness and separateness, two adults now enter into a re-formed bond as a couple. There is a silent or overt contract to support each other's growth and the growth of the relationship and to make it inclusive rather than exclusive. This receptive pattern allows input from others and from one's self to organize a layered existence, one that has room for many roles and interests. At this stage, each person has the chance to grow his or her somatic destiny and live it in a personal way with another partaking as he or she can. The deep internal feelings and values begin to find a narrative in the relationship, and find the means to body it. The relationship has become a separate somatic entity to which both adults contribute, giving and receiving from it as well as from each other. Here the relationship becomes a separate bodily entity that includes the two. They participate in a created environment that gives them a sense of being inside. The couple understands that the relationship requires care, concern, sharing, and intimacy. The adults are able to make themselves porous enough each to receive the other, but they have enough rigidity in their form to sustain their separate boundaries.

DIAGNOSTIC CATEGORIES

In somatic-emotional theory, two main diagnostic categories are used to look at couples and their patterns of interaction.

Underformed Patterns

The main characteristic of couples who fall into the *underformed* category is that they lack cohesive structures, firm boundaries and roles, and separate identities. Each partner wants to have most of his or her needs met by the other. These couples are in an engulfing pattern, which they confuse with intimacy or closeness.

There are two types of underformed relationships, swollen and porous.

Swollen couples have structures that are fragmented and inflated and their relationship is very stormy. Their needs and excitement are overcharged and urgent. They enact dramas of panic, of overwhelming or being overwhelmed; they are continuously in crisis. The new form that can emerge from this pattern is generally exploded or disorganized.

Porous couples have trouble sustaining excitement, both as individuals and together. Their structures are distended, with little form or rigidity. The partners merge and cling to each other. They enact dramas of neediness and rescue. Dreams may abound, but the capacity to translate them into sustained action is meager.

Overformed Patterns

Other couples are in relationships that are *overformed*; these patterns of relating are rigid and compacted, leaving no room for expansive feelings. In these relationships, receptivity is diminished. The result is feelings of isolation, alienation, aloneness, and dissatisfaction.

These partners live in compartments. They hunger for closeness and individuality as well as tenderness and intimacy, but do not know how to use themselves bodily to form both.

There are two types of overformed relationships, the rigid and the dense.

Rigid couples connect excitement with performance. They enact relationship by doing things together, either in side-by-side activities, or in dramas of competition.

Dense, compacted couples form relationships that congeal arousal so that emotions are dampened. Their relationships tend to end explosively, destabilizing what was stable and had meaning.

THE BODYING PRACTICE

The method used in formative therapy is the Bodying Practice; there are five stages. The primary goal of the work is to develop the skills to grow a personal emotional reality. Its aim is to help people form an emotional relationship that is congruent with their body structure. This is accomplished by helping them to experience their own somatic organization and process–*how* they use themselves physically, mentally, and emotionally.

The five Steps of the Bodying Practice may be summarized as follows:

Step One: To experience and recognize a particular somatic posture and relationship.

Step Two: To volitionally freeze-frame and isolate an aspect of the relationship configuration by stiffening or compressing the shape.

Step Three: To volitionally and slowly disassemble the over-organized form. This is critical to learning how to manage endings.

Step Four: To bodily learn to wait, and be receptive to one's body and one's partner's nonverbal answers.

Step Five: To volitionally reassemble a form and continue to practice it.

The Bodying Practice is based on the observation that the cortex participates in the process of forming a personal relationship with oneself and with another. This requires direct physical experience of one's own organizing process. The exercises are a means for developing the volitional abilities of the cortex to influence one's own behavior and to make emotional distinctions.

CASE EXAMPLE

Presenting Situation

Tom and Flora, both in their early 40s, have three children and came for therapy because both were in considerable distress about their relationship, which they described as being "out of control." No matter how much Flora reassured him, Tom never felt she really loved him, and he was wildly jealous of her relationships with other people, especially her brother, with whom he sometimes accused her of being sexually involved. Prior to seeking therapy, they had experienced an escalation in their fighting pattern; long sessions of Tom grilling Flora were turning first into screaming fights, and then into physical battles. Flora was quite frightened of Tom, and Tom was quite suspicious of her.

Somatic Structures

Tom was a powerfully built mesomorph, an action person, with a dense structure. His dense structure was a compensation for his swollen and inflamed inner excitement. There was an aura around him of tremendous inner intensity and a sense of being unpredictable.

Flora had a mesomorph's body also but it was unformed through lack of self-assertion. Her body was porous, yielding and looked like it was in a state of sinking in, collapsing. She appeared to be expending tremendous effort to hold herself together, literally making herself stiff to shore herself up.

Couple Dynamics

Tom and Flora had a uterine bond, one in which Tom was powerful and dominated a yielding and undemanding Flora. This bond had formed very rapidly when they had come together as emotionally unformed people, each seeking someone to complete his or her somatic-emotional deficits. They had enjoyed their engulfing bond for many years. Both had powerful reasons for feeling threatened at the prospect of ending this way of being a couple. Tom had grown up in a series of foster homes, and, for him, there were only two kinds of relationship situation: either you're engulfed or you're abandoned. Flora had grown up in the shadow of bullying, rejecting parents, experiencing herself as a small, intimidated, unformed adult child who, if she made no demands, was given a sense of being cared for; however, she had to be subservient to her world of adults. One can imagine the effect that a swollen, inflammable adult has on a small person. Flora told us that at first she loved being engulfed by Tom because it made her feel wanted and important.

Over the years of their marriage, Tom's possessive, demanding stance with Flora intensified, and Flora's shrinking and collapsing intensified reciprocally. Tom was dominated more and more by his own pattern of uncontrolled, intense self-pressuring and his longing for relief. His dense defense exploded at Flora. For Flora, yielding or disappearing was a way to let the emotional storms of anger or sexuality pass through. Flora, with her lack of form, had a shifting, mercurial identity that reinforced Tom's sense of abandonment. In effect, both had abandoned their adult forming and maturing process. They could not be there bodily or emotionally for themselves or for each other. They did not even consider growing and forming, or changing roles; being big and dominant, being the one in control, getting wanted responses, or yielding and being unformed were their respective goals.

Therapy Process

In the early sessions, Tom's intensely pressured dense and swollen presence filled the room. It was a courtroom scene, with a cowering Flora on trial and we, the therapists, assigned the roles of judge and jury. Tom demanded that the sessions be a forum for pursuing his complaints and investigating his suspicions about Flora. We encouraged Tom to disorganize his bullying body stance and learn to contain his excitement rather than push it on others. Flora we encouraged to stiffen her spine and limbs to not yield and to learn to take a stance rather than disappear. In this process, Tom and Flora learned to help each other. This was a formative partnership.

The inhibited excitement of this couple's engulfing bond had excluded everyone but themselves. In the ongoing work process, we helped them to somatically identify, experience, and disorganize and reorganize their major somatic-emotional patterns. We focused on working with Tom's dense, compacted body and with Flora's shrinking, unformed body. This work changed the dynamics of their relationship. First, it established a formative bond–a different way to be together, to share their bodies and be intimate. When Flora could fill herself out by stiffening, Tom's fears of being abandoned diminished, and with them the feelings that he needed always to be strong. He softened and received her assertive stiffening, which allowed her to have a presence and an independent body identity.

Flora's work involved strengthening her unformed adult to keep her adult shape from collapsing. Tom worked cooperatively to re-form his dense, swollen adult and to discover his right size. Influencing their respective somatic postures enabled them to form a more adult relationship.

When Flora focused her attention on her somatic state, she and we learned that she could not sense her lower body. It was as if she had no legs. Tom also found that he was all chest and neck, arms and face, with little feeling in his legs. Their reciprocal stance was for him to pull his body up and for her to shrink as a way to be present. In the sessions, we used the Bodying Practice Step Two (to intensify) to have her make form in her legs and pelvis. We had Tom disorganize his density using Step Three (to disassemble) and Step Four (to contain). Then he could let himself descend into his lower body and feel that he could fill himself.

Reorganization of the Couple's Bonding Pattern

We helped this couple use their bodies to organize a bond that permitted attachment and separateness, receptivity and support. By learning these somatic-emotional skills to influence their behavior, Tom and Flora participated in their own and each other's forming process.

CONCLUSIONS

Formative Psychology is about the life of the body and the body's relationships. The formative, somatic-emotional approach is aimed at helping people learn how to influence their somatic emotional patterns and form themselves as adults. It requires a high degree of commitment to the task of discovering how they are using themselves bodily.

We have an innate urge to body ourselves with others; a couple relationship is a bodily process. When couples seek professional help, it is because they are not able to influence their adult selves–which are either stunted or are not growing–and are, therefore, unable to mature their relationships. They are caught in the conflict between their urge to protect their experience of bodily coherence and stability that comes from maintaining the identity formed in their relationship, and their urge to grow themselves and their relationship. Not knowing how to reorganize themselves for the next stage of adult life, they experience somatic-emotional anxiety, persistent anger, helplessness, and depression.

Formative work helps partners cooperatively form a mutually supportive relationship, one grounded in a somatic-emotional system. In our experience, enabling partners to reorganize their body bonding patterns with each other deepens and matures their own bodily existence and their relationship, generating intimacy, feeling, and meaning.

Touch in Psychotherapy

Pauline Rose Clance
Earl C. Brown

SUMMARY. This article is an edited transcript of several experienced psychotherapists participating in an open dialogue on their personal experiences and thoughts regarding the use of touch in psychotherapy. They discuss the decision-making process in whether to apply or withhold touch, which includes several contextual variables such as timing, self-awareness of the therapist, countertransference, and the congruency between the appropriateness of the request for touch by the patient during the session and his or her own historical background. The usefulness of touch in psychotherapy is addressed. *[Article copies available for a fee from The Haworth Document Delivery Service: 1-800-342-9678. E-mail address: <getinfo@haworthpressinc.com> Website: <http://www.HaworthPress. com> © 2001 by The Haworth Press, Inc. All rights reserved.]*

KEYWORDS. Touch, body, psychotherapy, contact, healing, Satir

We, as psychotherapists, think it is important to discuss the issue of touch in psychotherapy as a result of the varied experiences that confront the therapist. There are some theoreticians and clinicians who state and believe one should never touch a client and there are others of us who think touch may be powerful in the healing process. We believe touch can be wisely and judiciously applied during the course of therapy to the benefit of our clients.

Pauline Rose Clance, PhD, is an editorial board member, *Journal of Couples Therapy*, and Professor of Psychology, Georgia State University, Atlanta, Georgia.

Earl C. Brown, PhD, is Professor of Psychology, Georgia State University, Atlanta, Georgia.

[Haworth co-indexing entry note]: "Touch in Psychotherapy." Clance, Pauline Rose, and Earl C. Brown. Co-published simultaneously in *Journal of Couples Therapy* (The Haworth Press, Inc.) Vol. 10, No. 2, 2001, pp. 61-73; and: *Couples and Body Therapy* (ed: Barbara Jo Brothers) The Haworth Press, Inc., 2001, pp. 61-73. Single or multiple copies of this article are available for a fee from The Haworth Document Delivery Service [1-800-342-9678, 9:00 a.m. - 5:00 p.m. (EST). E-mail address: getinfo@haworthpressinc.com].

The therapist's decision-making process in whether to apply or withhold touch in psychotherapy is a complex one where contextual variables, as well as the client and therapist as people, are critical. When experienced within an ethical context, touch may be used in a manner that minimizes its potential abuses and maximizes its potential benefits.

In the following discussion, several psychotherapists have joined together to share and discuss their personal experiences and views of with whom, when, and how touch may be used in the healing process and when touch may not be helpful. This transcript is an audio recording of an ongoing dialogue that has been transcribed and edited for written form.

Pauline Rose Clance, PhD, Interviewer: I am writing a chapter in a book on the decision-making process of the therapist in regard to touch. How do you decide who to touch or who not to touch? What kind of process, either at the more conscious or unconscious level, do you think is going on in this decision? And then I was interested in the differences, as you think about it, between patients you touch and patients you do not touch. Is that choice based on certain characteristics in the patient or not? Or more in general, what do you know about that decision in yourself. How do you decide with each person sitting there in front of you whether to touch or to not touch?

Earl C. Brown, PhD: There's one thing I know: It's not a question of touch to me; it's a question of what is good psychotherapy. It seems to me that touch has to be part of good psychotherapy, particularly if it's being done in a way that is described by words like humanistic, existential, experiential, gestalt, transactional, interpersonal, and broadly psychodynamic.

As far as I'm concerned, it's a patient-driven phenomenon. When a new person comes in, I'm acutely aware of them. I notice how close they walk to me, or how they pick out where they sit, or how they are in terms of posture. I recall one guy who startled me. The first time I saw him, he wanted to give me a great big hug. Then I learned, quite a bit later, that he did that because he heard I was a humanistic therapist, and he thought they did that a lot.

But the kinds of signs I'm looking for are how tense somebody is with me, or how relaxed they are. How much they seem to trust me versus how much they don't. Or how much there's a civility, which is pretty superficial, or cordiality, which goes some deeper. I do not make the first move or the first touch. I wait for that. If the patient sticks out their hand to shake, I shake hands. If a patient, maybe later on, wants a hug on the way out, fine. Sometimes (more often with men than women), I'll join in an arm around the shoulder or something like that.

And then there are people I've seen for a long time, and we're just cuddly-bums. One patient, for instance, reported that a friend asked her about seeing me and wondered why she came to see me. And the patient replied, "I wanna get held!" It was reparative of early trauma, but that was the reason she was coming, and I held her, at her request. I am comfortable holding someone who needs more than talk. Usually, I sit in the corner of my couch and place a pillow in my lap. If the patient stirs, I open my arms so they are free to shift, or to get up, and to move to another place.

There are some signs that will warn me off. One is if the person seems somewhat schizophrenic or paranoid or dissociated or something in the direction of multiple personality. I'm very slow to touch them, if at all, because I cannot expect a cohesive response; one part might be gratified while another is outraged.

Something else deserves to be mentioned here. I'm pretty good about getting touched elsewhere than in therapy sessions. So when I come to work, I'm not craving touch. While I thrill at touch, and I like the touch that I have with you-all, I don't look to a patient for touch. I'm usually pretty well satisfied on body contact.

There's another kind of patient who, as we go along in psychotherapy, allows their self to become dependent. And that to me is a good sign during the course of therapy; if they will allow themselves to depend upon me. The very conditions of psychotherapy, that is, exclusive attention, careful listening, empathetic understanding, and judicious responding, altogether, have a regressive inclination and attraction to them. If the patient feels safe enough to yield to this attraction, their dependency permits touching in a parent/child sort of way, figuratively bringing the child out to their skin. This contrasts with, and is corrective of, the real-life hurting events, which drove them further inside their body. The evidence is now clear: If kids are not touched in a loving way, they do not thrive; rather, they manifest a wasting away, a moroseness.

If a patient is dealing with something that is very difficult for them and they pat the couch beside them, I will move to sit beside them. The extent of physicality varies with my patient. Given certain circumstances, I have arm-wrestled with a patient; I have physically restrained a patient from leaving my office in a deranged state; I required one patient to wear a motorcycle helmet because he would lunge at the wall as a way of punishing himself for bad thoughts.

Also, if I surmise that a patient is accustomed to having a "sucker parent," or wants to make me into Dr. Feelgood, I would rather not physically comfort or console them at that time. It's better that I help them to become aware of their resistance to whatever is in the offing.

It is important that–if I touch a patient in an extraordinary way–it has to be clear that this is *not* sex. And it also has to be clear that we can talk about it. For instance, if somebody asks me to hold them (and I do hold them), at the next session I will go back to that holding and talk about it to find out how that felt to them, or what followed upon that, or if they have any concerns or worries, or if it brought up anything in particular. So, we process that. A lot of body stuff is silent. A lot of feelings and movements don't have words, especially if somebody was messed up very early in life. What I want to do is to get that conscious and one way of getting it conscious is to refer to it, reflect upon it, and to talk about it.

There are times when it *is* sex. Times when I feel myself being seduced. The patient's agenda is not the same as my own. Far from touch, all I want to do is take notice. Why does this man gaze intently into my eyes; why does this woman come dressed and comport herself in this manner? I suppose that it is already conscious on their part. I need to get equally conscious on my part. Without blame or shame, we need to get to the place where we can talk about it and fit it into the pattern of their life. Often, it turns out, seduction is an effort to turn therapy into something other than therapy; a turning-of-a-table that was encountered earlier in their life when a caretaker turned into an abuser. If the therapist colludes in the seduction, and both act out their fantasies, then therapy is at an end. The therapist is disgraced and the patient goes on as before, without trust, perhaps some revenge, but no resolution.

Touch is too valuable at connecting to be severed from practice and its value is preserved when the therapist can discern the trauma of disrupted relationships and not add another link to the chain.

Debbara J. Dingman, PhD: I had two reactions, Earl: one was to your statement about the patient who allows himself or herself to become dependent in the course of psychotherapy, and how that is a good sign. The current Zeitgeist is shaming about that aspect of psychotherapy. Managed care companies look at the bottom line, symptom reduction, and short-term treatment. From within that paradigm, to say that the therapist is fostering dependency is to pronounce the ultimate shaming dismissal of the therapeutic relationship. So our discussion is healing to me. Those who categorically declare that dependency and physical contact have no place in psychotherapy propose that we are born dependent and that our goal in life is to become independent, or not dependent. This is not true. In contrast, our discussion reflects our understanding that one develops over time and, in psychotherapy, from infantile dependency to mature, adult dependency. One could also call it mutuality or interdependency or something like that.

I was thinking about an appointment that I had this morning. The man asked me to hold him, and I did not want to. I'm wondering if it's about the issue of dependency. He does not want to be dependent on me. There is also something very hostile in our interaction. He was very controlling and particular throughout the session, insisting that I not speak. Then he said, "Will you please come hold me and comfort me?" I suggested that we talk about it instead.

So we did that, and I did not touch him in the session. It intuitively felt wrong to have physical contact when our emotional contact was so jagged and unexplored. Previously with this man, I had made a clear decision to have physical contact with him in a group setting, but not alone in my office. I do not know quite how to explain that clinically.

Dr. Brown: You don't need to. What is happening in me is how you as a person feel about this want. And I would take that seriously–how you feel–like I don't want to. Not to violate your kid, because probably your kid is saying I don't want to.

Interviewer: Earl, in response to your statement that touch must be patient-driven and that the therapist must also be self-aware, I recall that one of our former graduate students reported the following:

I remember an important lesson I learned (it only took once) about timing with a patient of mine. In the first session I held her, comforted her. My supervisor very kindly said, "You may have to deal with that later on," and boy was she right. It created a dynamic that was premature and not workable. It was really tough to move out of that kind of good-mother pose that was driven by me, not by the patient.

It created an unhealthy dependency where the work was blocked, effectively, for quite some time. Then with my trying to extricate (you know, having to do my own work), it just botched it for a long time. I mean one horrible experience that was not fun or pleasant–or more importantly, not necessarily therapeutic all the way around. The patient got the early impression that I was going to do it for them. Now one of my big parameters is taking time to know the person, because even after three months sometimes I'm not sure what the signals are about.

Dan Mermin, PhD: Here's the crux of what I think. I certainly find that, overall, I touch patients less than I did 15 years ago. That partly comes out of the climate and partly it comes out of my own experience. In general, I wait for a patient's cues. I'm also clear that with some clients I immediately put my hand out when I first meet them in the waiting room and at the end of that first session. And it seems fine. But there are some times I don't; I wait. I feel like that is kind of instinctive. So far, I'm trusting that. I haven't violated anyone or set up some kind of dynamic by doing that, which says to me I'm processing pretty well what I'm getting. I do have people with whom I have not even shaken hands. Somehow I pick up on a cue about that. I'm sure that on certain days it has more to do with how I am that day, but I think I'm also responsive to what they're putting out.

I think that my views about touch have been very much influenced by my training in psychomotor–kind of in both directions in the sense that psychomotor gave me a structure for making touch safer for people (in group setting, in particular), so that I'm quite comfortable with it. I know that part of the procedure is that I'll be checking with them at every step. You know, do you want contact or not? And how does that touch feel and do you want that hand on your hand or not, etc.?

That guides me to a degree with individual clients, in a sense, that I may do a piece of what you call a psychomotor structure. It's what you call a one-on-one with a client, usually with a cushion, an object, or occasionally using the cushion as an ideal figure, a negative figure, but then I'll be an extension of that figure in some way. For example, someone's working with a different kind or a positive kind of father and mother. We may use a cushion for that figure, and then I'll be an extension of that. So sometimes I will be holding someone, once removed with the big pillow between us, where I'm just supplying the backup work.

I've also been a containment figure for people's rage or aggression, again using a cushion as a kind of buffer. I have people push into a cushion and try to push it through the wall with me standing behind it. Just push with their fist or push with their shoulder in such a way that they feel the solidity of containment. So psychomotor has kind of given me some techniques for doing touch in a way that feels clearly defined.

Dr. Brown: Symbolic.

Dr. Mermin: Right, exactly.

Interviewer: In a group setting.

Dr. Mermin: Yes, but what I was describing was one-on-one. In a group setting I use other group members. Then I'm much more comfortable, say, about having a positive parent hold someone directly. In general, I do that in sessions. I hug people sometimes at the end of the session, and I have sat with people with my arm around them at times, but it's pretty infrequent. Some of the time there is deep grief or falling apart, and, in some instances, I may provide that with their permission. I probably do that less than I used to. Or, I'm more inclined to extend a hand or something–a hand to hold if they want it rather than sitting beside them. Probably the only exceptions to that in the last few years have been with a very severely dissociative client who moved into flashbacks and was thrashing about in the room, banging her head against the wall, stuff like that. I have physically restrained a client and held her, but then with a lot of processing afterwards.

I want to share with you that I also wrote to an insurance company about touch. It probably was not as thorough as the statement I just made (Note: an insurance company had asked, "Do you touch clients" and Dr. Mermin had written a statement about touch to them).

Dr. Brown: You know I put out that one-sentence thing on consent to touch. All it said was: "I consent to being touched–in a nonsexual way–by my therapist during our sessions." And I got some feedback, particularly from Pauline. I'm going to lengthen that; I'm going to add some more stuff. Perhaps I can pick up something from what you had to say that would help me in adding to my consent form.

Dr. Mermin: I found it was very interesting. I know I must be very comfortable with it because I was irritated about writing the statement, but I also felt very clear that I was going to own what I did. I didn't feel apologetic.

And then the feedback I got from the insurance company was: "yes, we agree with you for this year." And I didn't submit a release form, but the company said: "we think you would be safer if you had your client sign a release form." But they didn't say you have to do this.

Interviewer: That is one of the things I was thinking might be helpful, that is, that we come up with some kind of consent form regarding touch. And it's also part of a way of educating clients. So that's something I've been thinking about a lot as I'm getting feedback from therapists and clients. One of the interesting things is that people who are very much identified as body psychotherapists indicate that in some ways they feel less struggle about touching and when to touch and how to touch because they think that people come to them with this clear notion that they're going to work with their body. I began to wonder if, in part, gaining an informed consent from clients, or educating them in some kind of consent form, about touch might be helpful–something like, "From time to time, I may find that touch is an important therapeutic tool" and "With your consent" or "With your request." The wording would be very important, I think. But it's interesting that the body therapists don't have a specific consent form, but they indicate that they think they have an implicit contract because they label themselves body therapists.

Bruce Pemberton, PhD: Well, I think they do. Increasingly, I find myself referring people who I feel would benefit from a lot of touch to body therapists or massage therapists. I've done that about four times in the last year in conjunction with what we're doing in our therapy. I have gone from touching a lot in the early work I did 15 or 20 years ago to hardly touching at all now. Any touch I do is clearly patient-driven, and usually a handshake or a hug, although I haven't hugged a patient in a long time.

Ruth Hepler, PhD: Even at the end of a session?

Dr. Pemberton: Right. What I found over time is that the patient who wanted a hug would ask for it on rare occasions after I stopped offering it. I used to do it for me as much as for the patient and over time got all supervised out of that. As I got more in tune with the patient's needs, I found I didn't want as much hugging. I don't know if I want it or don't want it now, but I just don't hug as much anymore. What I didn't like before in both groups and individual psychotherapy was that once people hug it becomes an expectation and, therefore, an obligation. When we talked about that in groups, some people always expressed this sense of obligation to hug or touch and relief at opening up the subject. In recent years in group, I look at when people touch and ask people to talk about their touching in the group. I ask people to put in words what they were trying to express by their touch.

In couples group there is a lot of touching which is really important to find an expression in words. One person might be saying something and continue to go on and on, and the other partner will put their hand out and touch their arm. Or one person might come in late and somebody will say something to them, and they'll reach out and grab their partner's hand. There is always valuable information behind the touch, and I want the group to discover the meaning behind the touch.

I don't shake hands much anymore, because if it's not extended I don't want to initiate. Yet I notice I do sometimes stick out my hand, which I just realized is almost always with a couple. It's usually a male, and it's usually a certain kind of male, and I feel quite comfortable. But not shaking is usually my pattern because, after that initial time, at the end of the session, I will wait for the extended hand. And most people don't offer then.

I wonder what the cues are for me to initiate the handshake. I know I wait for his approach. How a person gets up from a chair in the waiting room and how quickly they come forward tells me if they are expecting a handshake. There is a cue there. Even if the hand is not extended, the quality is partly in the rate and it's partly in the eye contact.

So I think more and more of asking patients to put their touch into words, and, when I feel someone needs holding, I don't do the work of holding. I love referring folks either for a period of time or for simultaneous therapy to people I've come to trust and appreciate to do that. It's just like anything else. I'll refer when others do something better than I do. There are things that I don't do that well, and I will refer patients to people who are more comfortable or used to touching, and whom I feel know their boundaries perhaps better than I know mine. That's been an evolutionary thing.

I don't think it has to do as much with the times; I think it has to do with my own personal therapeutic work. Almost all my own therapy work in my life right now has to do with body therapy. It's interesting that I do less touching as I get touched more. When I think of doing body work, and I have considered this, I think of doing it more formally and getting trained in it. I appreciate people who are well trained. And when I make a referral to a body therapist, the patient has set to be touched. And when I go to a body therapist I expect a contract to be touched.

I also realize that in my own therapy I didn't get a lot of touching. So I think that sticks in my expectation.

And I think the thing I learned most about responding to the client's need or checking for permission to touch came from Virginia Satir. I just love watching the way she would enter somebody's personal spaces. She would say, "My hand is on the edge of your chair here. I have an urge to touch your arm. Would that be alright with you?" She would always say, "I really have the urge to touch your throat or to pinch your toes. What do you think of that?" She would always announce and receive permission.[1] If she did not receive permission, she was very lovely, staying right there. She didn't withdraw. It wasn't like, "Oh, well, you don't want me to touch you there." She would say, "This is probably the right distance for now." Just constantly communicating her urge to initiate or responding to the other person's request or urge.

I think I touch less now than I used to, because I think I'm less sure of always announcing my intention or getting permission at this point. So when you circulated the consent form, I realize now I will probably read it again. I like what you're doing, and I'm thinking: Do I want to add that back in? Most of the touching I have done in my work with clients was either holding or touching the chest, the throat, or the face.

Interviewer: Sort of a way to help a person release?

Dr. Pemberton: Right. But I do that seldom now. For a while, I found people less and less expressive. Now I don't see that much difference. I see people feeling safe and coming to real sobbing and crying, through silence, or from just a word or an observation about how they are holding themselves or not breathing. I often have them touch their own chest. When I have an urge to touch their chest now, I might ask them to watch their hands and follow their hand to their chest and put a little more pressure on their chest, or throat, and see what happens.

Interviewer: That's a good tip.

Dr. Pemberton: I was thinking if I see some symptoms, I might say, "I'm wondering if you want someone there beside you" or "I'm wondering if there is a yearning about having or inviting someone to be there to hold you." I might personalize it and check to see if they would like me to be there. And almost always now it comes to either a gestalt or some kind of self-work on their past. I guess I don't ask them for permission to touch–I don't want to initiate. I take my impulses and try to look for what this involves, put it out there for them to activate.

Dr. Mermin: What struck me with Pesso (founder of psychomotor psycho-therapy) is noticing the part I call self-touching where the person is doing his or her own self-soothing.[2] He always uses that, as a cue for introducing the outside figure.

Dr. Pemberton: That's right.

Dr. Mermin: And you're saying you can go the other way.

Dr. Pemberton: Um hum.

Dr. Mermin: You can do it with cues, too, or actively self-sooth.

Dr. Pemberton: Or I'll find the figure . . .

Dr. Mermin: That you want. And then, in effect, you're still the symbolic, outside figure just observing. It's interesting. It's their hand, you know. I often use my urge to touch as information. I have the tendency towards what Virginia might do, but really I hardly ever touch any more.

Dr. Dingman: In a recent session, a client was crying and patting herself. The motion of her hands was unusual for her, and I was intrigued by it. I asked if she could tell me what her hand was saying. At the time, I thought she ignored my question and I let it go. My fantasy was that her hand was expressing her request for contact.

She started the next session saying, "I want to talk about my hand." Terrific. She said, "I couldn't answer your question last week but I wanted you to hold my hand." This opened up new areas in her psychotherapy. We spoke for the next few sessions about her not being able to ask me, about her not being able to answer my question, about her wish for me to hold her hand, about her fantasies about why I didn't, and what all of that means in the context of her life.

At the end of the period of processing all of that, she made the following request: "I want to make this explicit that the next time you see my body communicating something that I cannot put into words and you have a hunch about what I'm saying to you, will you please act on your hunch. I promise we'll hang in there to process it through completely and to a positive outcome later." I agreed to take that risk with her. So that's where we are in her therapy, because she is asking for that right now.

Interviewer: Sounds like a great contract.

Dr. Dingman: We'll see where we go.

Dr. Hepler: Except I would probably (even with that) tell her what my fantasy was. Instead of acting on it I think. I would probably negotiate my part and say, "Well I think I'd rather say something" when she would say, "No, I want you to act on it."

Dr. Dingman: Well, what I've said is, I will verbally mediate it, as I did, and our contract is now if she is still not verbally responding, I will move toward. I will take some risk. And then in our contract, we will process this after that. Fine tune until we get it.

Dr. Hepler: It makes me think about how we haven't used this word yet, but we've all alluded to it: about how we use *countertransference* in our work around touch. We've used the term *patient-driven* a lot, but I am almost equally aware of my own countertransference. I know when I've had patients and have been aware of some sexual excitement on my part. That's a real clear sign for me to be very careful about any kind of touch.

When you talked about Virginia Satir, that's the way I work. I don't know that I got it from her, but if I feel that countertransference, I make it conscious by saying, "I'm aware that I'm feeling like coming and sitting beside you." I just make it a statement. Not "May I," or "Should I?" And they'll usually say, "That would feel good," or "That would be scary."

And also at the end of sessions sometimes, when a person has been real hostile and there's been negative energy in a session and they want a hug, I will say, "I don't think our energy today really supports that, and we'll talk about it next week because what it feels like is an old aggressive, unhealthy dynamic of 'let's kiss and make up' and it never works." So I've been really aware of how important my feelings are about touch, and then processing afterwards.

Another thing I've been aware of with patients is how *they* make touch an issue. There's a person I'm working with right now who, in times past, earlier in her work, I did some much-needed holding with her. She's moved along really quite beautifully in her process and doesn't require that now. Not that getting away from touch means health, but for her it was progressive. We had a session recently where she had really been through a bad time. And she said in the session, "I was aware that at some point today I wanted to have you just come over here and just hold me." And I thought to myself, "That would not be the best thing for me right now." And that just felt like . . .

Dr. Brown: . . . that she could get to that.

Dr. Hepler: Absolutely, and that she put the break on it herself.

Interviewer: I thank each of you for discussing this issue and for your thoughts about touch in psychotherapy.

The use of touch in psychotherapy is an important and relevant therapeutic modality that can contribute to positive therapeutic change and growth when applied appropriately. One common viewpoint held by these psychotherapists is that touch is a patient-driven phenomenon. Careful observations of the client's own physical behavior toward the therapist is assessed as a cue, which reflects the receptivity or inclination for therapeutic touch. More often than not, it is a client's verbal request for touch which initiates the use of touch by the therapist. When touch occurs, it is important to constantly "check-in," discuss, and process the experience. However, if a therapist thinks touch can benefit a client, for instance, to help facilitate getting in touch with his or her feelings, the therapist asks permission and then explains the procedure. The creation of a consent form for a client's permission for touch may be helpful for therapists who use touch as an integral part of their therapy work.

Whether touch is client or patient-driven, several contextual variables influence the therapist's decision-making process. Some considerations are timing, the presence or lack of congruency between the appropriateness of the request for touch in relation to the client's dynamic background or the emotional milieu of the session, and the therapist's self-knowledge of his or her own boundaries. Despite theoretical criticisms, it is the discussants' belief that touch may be appropriate and beneficial for a client's development of a healthy, adult dependency in the therapeutic relationship. In some instances, however, touch may be counterproductive, especially when the expectation for touch has been established early in the relationship and later, inadvertently, evolves into an ungrounded obligation. At other times, for example, when the client's expression for touch appears to be sexual in nature, it is the responsibility of the therapist to discern and deal with the client's possible acting out behavior of previous abuse situations and *definitely not touch the client.* Processing what is happening seems much more crucial.

Overall, the general attitude by the psychotherapists is that touch may be important within good psychotherapy. The beneficial effects of touch may also be achieved through indirect means. This may include a therapist's guidance and observation of client self-soothing and affective self-reflection or the client's verbal interpretation of his/her desire for touch. Whether touch is utilized or not, it is important for both the client and therapist to process such issues in the therapy.

A call for further research and ongoing inter-dialogue among licensed professionals is needed to help therapists further address questions, resolve ambiguity, guide, and demystify the use of touch by therapists in the therapeutic context. In *Touch in Psychotherapy*[3] these issues are discussed in several different chapters.

NOTES

1. Satir, V. (1967). *Conjoint family therapy.* Palo Alto, CA: Science and Behavior Books.

2. Pesso, A. (1973). *Experience in action.* New York: New York University Press.

3. Smith, E.W.L., Clance, P.R., & Imes, S. (1998). *Touch in psychotherapy: Theory, research, and practice.* New York: The Guilford Press.

Body Psychotherapy with Couples: Using the Seven Developmental Stages Model of Bodynamic Analysis

Anne Isaacs

Joel Isaacs

SUMMARY. Bodynamic Analysis combines depth cognitive psycho-therapy and an emphasis on relationship with an understanding of the body based on an empirical study of the psychological function of each muscle. The resulting developmental understanding has been elaborated in the form of Seven Developmental Stages, each having specific themes and issues. These themes and issues are often found to be at the core of the conflictual dynamics presented by couples who are seeking therapy. Thus, while addressing the issues of one person, we can simultaneously be eliciting and working with the interpersonal dynamics of the couple. *[Article copies available for a fee from The Haworth Document Delivery Service: 1-800-342-9678. E-mail address: <getinfo@haworthpressinc.com> Website: <http://www.HaworthPress.com> © 2001 by The Haworth Press, Inc. All rights reserved.]*

KEYWORDS. Body psychotherapy, Bodynamic Analysis, developmental stages, developmental themes, character positions, resignation, touch

Recently, one of us was asked to participate in a panel on body psychotherapy with couples that was focused around a hypothetical vignette. We would like to use this vignette and our response to it as an introduction to how we

Anne Isaacs, LCSW, is on the Board of Directors of the United States Association of Body Psychotherapy and was co-chair of their recent conference. She is a Bodynamic Analyst and Trainer practicing in Los Angeles.

Joel Isaacs, PhD, a Bodynamic Analyst and Trainer, has been a Reichian therapist in Los Angeles for over 20 years. He has published numerous articles in *Energy and Character* and recently in *Bioenergetic Analyst*.

[Haworth co-indexing entry note]: "Body Psychotherapy with Couples: Using the Seven Developmental Stages Model of Bodynamic Analysis." Isaacs, Anne, and Joel Isaacs. Co-published simultaneously i *Journal of Couples Therapy* (The Haworth Press, Inc.) Vol. 10, No. 2, 2001, pp. 75-90; and: *Couples ar Body Therapy* (ed: Barbara Jo Brothers) The Haworth Press, Inc., 2001, pp. 75-90. Single or multiple copie of this article are available for a fee from The Haworth Document Delivery Service [1-800-342-9678, 9:00 a.n - 5:00 p.m. (EST). E-mail address: getinfo@haworthpressinc.com].

use our training as Bodynamic Analysts when we each work with couples. First, we'll give an overview, then say what we would scan for, and then discuss what our particular body psychotherapy perspective brings to this situation. We will then discuss the vignette and our response to it. Then we will present a case history that allows us to go into more practical detail about how we bring the client's body into psychotherapy.

OVERVIEW OF WORKING WITH COUPLES

Our personal and professional experience is that we all want intimacy but we are all simultaneously ambivalent about it, at least at some level. Intimacy is wonderful, and it can also be very disturbing since it can bring up too many feelings, especially strong early ones. This polarity, this push-pull, this structural contradiction, this cosmic dance is what brings many couples to therapy. One cornerstone of our Bodynamic approach is the concept that a central aspect of human life is the seeking of what we call "mutual connection." Most simply, the "mutual" part is conveyed by the question: "Can I be myself and still be connected to you?" It is our understanding that when there are stresses or breaks in mutual connection, the infant or child, in order to maintain or restore some connection, will distort himself in ways that lead to the patterns we see in adults. How these disturbances play out in later life is often the focus of our work with couples. Each person in a couple has qualities that the partner admires and would like for themselves. Often, some of our deeper issues and stronger feelings may only arise when we get close to someone, when we are intimate. And, at these times, it is often difficult to separate one's own issues from what is a reaction to the other person's behavior. We keep in mind that the issues and feelings couples bring in may not be ones they are familiar with or can presently own.

If we broaden our vision for a moment to examine the social context in which couples operate, we can see that individuals in our society generally come together as a couple to find love, peace, security, and fulfillment, and often to raise a family. Of these, the most widely talked about is love. When we ask people what love is, they often say love is a feeling, and it turns out to be a feeling that lacks a precise definition. But how is it that something so many people want can't easily be described? Perhaps this is one source of the difficulty in obtaining it. We are seeking, sometimes desperately, a feeling that cannot be precisely defined. (But, "You'll know it when you feel it.") Sadly, this definition of love as a feeling is only one part of love, some of the time.

Love is not an instinct that rises up in us, and love is not an emotion. Feelings always come and go, and we would not normally make a long-term commitment based on a feeling we know is temporary. Love encompasses acceptance, compassion, and empathy, and loving someone will help us to open our own heart. A fuller, deeper, more useful idea of love knows it as an act of will, a choice, a decision, a promise even. The practice of love is perhaps best understood as the will to extend oneself for the purpose of nurturing one's own or another person's spiritual growth. A loving relationship requires us to extend ourselves, to commit to open and honest expression and communication. It requires us to both show and expect: care, affection, respect, responsibility, commitment, and trust. Love is as love does.

How might a view of love as an action and an intention help individuals in a relationship or those that are seeking one? They could begin by seeing loving as a practice of putting their partner's interests on an equal footing with their own. They would understand that work and challenges will be involved if they are to maintain and deepen the connection made possible by their original connection. They might even come to see the appearance of difficulties as a possible sign that their relationship is *maturing,* for only in the embrace of intimacy is there space for early wounds to surface. There they are given an opportunity for healing each other's early wounds. They might even be able to recognize their struggles in this relationship as helping them to become the person they longingly hope to be. As therapists, we see this perspective as both helpful and motivational, both supportive and challenging, and we try to impart some of this vision to couples whenever we believe it is appropriate.

THE INITIAL SESSION

In the initial session, we believe the couple's first impression of their therapist is very important. Here they should be evaluating whether they feel seen and accepted. However, their evaluation of us will often have a component of each deciding "Whose side is he/she on?" Or, alternatively, out of fear of their own issues, they might find it safer to come together to reject us. So it is vital for each partner to have the experience of being heard and affirmed by the therapist. Secondarily, at whatever level they can take it in, it is of great value for each person to witness his/her partner being heard and affirmed. Perhaps they can begin to understand some of what the other needs and to witness the relaxation and decrease in tension that can occur for the partner when the partner's needs are fulfilled. This opens the door that separates their closed place of stuckness from the possibilities that lie outside.

There are many avenues that can be pursued at this point in the first session, and many of the initial impressions we get would go into making the choices. Often what they bring in may want some immediate attention. Sometimes an action or expression of one, or a dynamic between the two, will allow an entry to a core issue. Meanwhile, we try to assess their levels of commitment to each other and to the therapy process, their levels of intimacy and of self-awareness. We also try to assess each person's ability to stay connected with his/her center and his/her ability to maintain a boundary when in interaction. In the latter case, we might suggest they explore changing the distance between their seats so that they might better sense themselves clearly. We might want to focus on one and then the other, or we might want to have them engage in a dialog. We might bring in some physical action, or we might decide to keep the session verbal.

A BODYNAMIC ANALYTIC VIEW

But let us now move on to what is unique from our perspective of Bodynamic Analysis. The Bodynamic System combines depth cognitive psychotherapy, and an emphasis on relationship, with new research on the psychomotor development of children. The body is integrated into the therapy through a knowledge of the psychological function of each muscle. The resulting developmental understanding has been elaborated in a form usable by psychotherapists, a model of Seven Developmental Stages. This model is based on over twenty years of empirical research on how mind and body are connected. It contains a lot of specific information to be used as a guide. In work with couples, we would be very attuned to whether either or both partners were predominantly acting from one or perhaps two developmental stages. We would get clues from their body structure and posture (e.g., as they walk in, how they sit), their energy and vocal style, their choice of words and phrases, and, of course, from the issues that they raise and how they present them (e.g., Macnaughton, 1997). This information begins to direct our attention toward what we should suspect to be their underlying issues, and how we might respond to them. Their responses to our initial offerings tell us whether we are on the right track.

Let us devote a few pages to our character structure model of Seven Developmental Stages. A character structure model is a psychological description of a developmental stage and a guide to how difficulties encountered in infancy and childhood may be carried over into the present and influence adult functioning. Character structure has some of its roots in Freud's ideas about oral, anal, phallic, latency, and genital stages, and was later developed by Erik Erikson. Wilhelm Reich (1949), a student of Freud, worked with Freud's ideas and included more body characteristics for each stage. Further work from a body perspective was done by Alexander Lowen (1958, 1975) in the 50s and 60s. In these latter descriptions, character can be recognized from body posture and structure, as well as from attitudes, defenses, and issues presented in therapy. This early work sprang from the observation that when children are frustrated in an activity, they may develop a chronic tension in their muscles to hold back that activity. Working from a complementary direction, Lisbeth Marcher (1992) and her colleagues realized that flaccid or under-elastic muscles correspond to impulses, insights, and skills that are mostly absent or only partially learned. This, they found, is the body counterpart of psychological resignation.

One contribution of Bodynamic Analysis was to extend the character model to later years by identifying seven discrete developmental stages. Subsequent empirical research at the Bodynamic Institute, Denmark, linked each muscle with its psychomotor task and with the time in development when the muscle first comes under voluntary control. It is at this time that the elasticity of the muscle becomes imprinted (over-, under-, or normal elasticity). Since specific groups of muscles correspond to the developmental tasks of specific stages, it is possible to get an overall reading for each developmental stage. This led to the recognition that there are three possible positions for each stage and led to a greater clarity in the description and characteristics for each stage (see Bernhardt and Isaacs, 2000).

The seven developmental stages span the time from the second trimester of pregnancy through twelve years of age (Appendix 1, and Bernhardt et al., 1995, 1996). Each stage has some time overlap with the stage just before and just after it. And each stage has a predominant theme, from which it gets its name: Existence, Need, Autonomy, Will, Love/Sexuality, Opinion Forming, and Solidarity/Performance. If the infant or child's experience of his/her holding environment during a given stage is "good enough," the child will emerge more or less with the resources appropriate to that stage (the "resourced position"). For example, the Will Stage, which spans 2 to 4 years of age, has a major theme that can be expressed by the question: "Can I be focused, powerful, and expressive and still be loved and accepted in my family?" If the child's experience is good enough, he/she will be in the resourced position, which we characterize as "assertive." This child, and later this person, can use his or her abilities and power in appropriate ways.

If there are disruptions or disturbances to development that are severe, consistent, and/or early in that stage, the child will likely be in the "early position" for that stage. Very generally this means that not all of the resources to be learned here were acquired and that the child will be prone to experience resignation around the themes appropriate to that stage. If we again look at the Will Stage, we see that the early position is called "self-sacrificing." The child has learned that his/her strength was most welcomed when it was in the service of another person, usually a parent. A person operating from this position will often not know how to act appropriately in his or her own interest. Clients can be helped to awaken undeveloped impulses and skills, exactly the ones missing but needed for working through these specific developmental tasks. The therapist's ability to recognize and work directly with this psychological resignation by building new ego resources can be transformative.

On the other hand, if there are disruptions or disturbances that are not too severe or consistent, or that occur later in the stage, then the child will likely be in the "later position" for that stage. Again, generally, this means that the child has more of the energy and resources from this stage, but will tend to be rigid, fixed, or repetitive in the relevant behaviors and attitudes. For the Will Stage, this late position is called "judging." A child or adult acting from this position will will hold back his/her own power and often will be critical of others who show initiative. More generally, unless the unresolved issues from any stage are resolved at later developmental stages, during the teenage years, through life experience, or in therapy, the adult behavior will show aspects of these early or late position characterological patterns.

People in difficulty or under stress are very often acting from one or, in some cases, two character positions. When these positions are identified, we are often able to elucidate the underlying themes and issues more clearly and directly. One of the lovely advantages of using this model with couples is that there are well-known clashes leading to specific dynamics between people who are acting from certain positions. Thus, by addressing the issues of one person, we can often simultaneously be working with the interpersonal dynamics of the couple. Because of the specificity of the Bodynamic model, and our ability to use a person's body awareness along with simple movements to help bring forth the psychodynamics involved in most issues, we do not generally rely on exercises to do this.

THE VIGNETTE

Jenny burst into my office followed by Sam, who followed her to the couch. Speaking quickly, she described their long-term relationship and how it was way past time for them to get married and have children. He appeared to be slowly sinking into the couch as she spoke. When I asked how he was with all of this, he replied slowly that he didn't see any reason to rush this and why was she always in such a hurry. Her level of anxiety increased visibly as she heard this. By the time he was finished, she was sitting on the edge of her seat ready to spring. He looked very calm by contrast with his legs outstretched heavily sunk into the couch.

Applying Our Model to the Vignette

At first "glance" Jenny and Sam each seem to be coming, at least partly, from the earliest developmental stage. This stage, named the Existence level, is, in our view, where the fetus and infant determines whether or not the world is a welcoming, friendly, loving place (Lake, 1966, 1970). Since this stage is so early, its theme is very broad, and, at the same time, the means to deal with the environment are the least developed. Thus the infant's responses to a less than friendly environment are potentially the most drastic. If the environment is judged not to be welcoming enough, then the major protective mechanism available involves energetically splitting the mind-body unity into very different positions.

A person acting from the early position, we name it the Mental Existence position, has a predominantly mental view of the world. This position, especially in its extremes (and under stress), is characterized by a strong detachment from the world, an introversion, and a commitment anxiety. The other polarity is the Emotional Existence position. This position, especially in its extremes (and under stress), is characterized by a strong separation anxiety, an extroversion, and a compulsive need for contact. In our scenario, Jenny seems to be coming at least partly from the Emotional position, and Sam from the Mental position. Sam is also showing some characteristics of the early Autonomy position, which is characterized by non-verbal activity changing. Not being in touch with their own impulses and desires, a person acting from this position will often slow things down in order not to be swept up in another person's choices. So these would be our starting assumptions, and we would be checking continuously to affirm whether they were valid and to what extent. If our interventions help an individual or a couple to feel seen, contacted, or understood, if they enliven or calm a person or help them come forward in a new way, then we are probably on the right track. If this is not the case, we let go of the initial hypothesis and use the new clues we are getting to form another one. Let's assume for now that our assessments above about Sam and Jenny are roughly correct.

When first listening to Sam and Jenny, we would look for opportunities to affirm the qualities that led them to have a long-term relationship. And given the state Sam and Jenny are presently in, we would not overdo this. People showing the Mental and Emotional positions can be very attractive to each other, each having some of what the other is lacking. For example, the Mental is often seemingly very self-contained, and the Emotional seemingly very alive and in contact with the world. And we can see how this can lead to a negative feedback loop under stress, when Jenny strains for attachment and Sam for detachment. So, in session we would try to give Jenny the emotional contact we believe she needs and wants. We would also try be very concrete and factual in exchanges with her. By contrast, while making some contact with Sam, we would also give him lots of space. We would first try to meet him at an abstract level and talk about his ideas of what is going on between them. If this is successful, we would then edge toward exploring his impulses and feelings.

Whenever we might sense or perceive something going on with Sam, we would draw his attention to the sensation in his body or a specific part of his body. In this way, we would hope to help him contact what he is feeling, along with what he is thinking. If he passively resists something Jenny or the therapist says, we would try to help him discover his own feelings or ideas beneath this. We would look for opportunities to be supportive, first verbally, and, as appropriate, by either asking him to put tension in the muscles that correspond to support for this developmental stage, or by stimulating the muscle ourselves (see Appendix 2). In general, we understand that a person in the earlier position in any stage needs more support, while a person in the later stage, having more energy and resources from that stage, can accept more challenge.

By contrast, with Jenny, we would affirm her feelings and make contact with her at an emotional level. We would begin to show her and teach her ways to contain her feelings, which seem to have a strong effect on Sam and sometimes might overwhelm her also. We would help her to center so that her feelings would be more connected to her thoughts. This could be approached either by having her bring her awareness to her inner abdominal area or by asking her to put some tension into the muscles we have determined relate to centering (Bernhardt and Isaacs, 2000). When we had done these things, and when emotional contact was made, wherever appropriate, we would help her to understand the reasoning behind her feelings and follow the reasoning to its conclusions, being aware that sometimes this might be fear-provoking (and, therefore, ordinarily avoided). We would pay attention to clarifying the feelings and thoughts contained in any of her expressions that were meta-phorical, because the latter can be a source of confusion to herself and of misunderstanding with her partner.

As some of the tension between Sam and Jenny softened, and where appropriate, when giving contact to one (or contact with space to the other), we would turn to the other partner and ask how it is for them when their partner asks them for connection (or space). In this way we would hope to help each person begin to sense how it is for the other when they try to get what they hope for and so desperately want. Here, without naming it, we have begun to work with the dynamic between them that is likely most problemat-ic. As we connect the past (character structure) with the present (feelings, attitudes, issues, dynamics), we are forming an implicit trajectory leading into the future. Couples can begin to sense new possibilities opening to them as they have new experiences and acquire new resources related to the issues and conflicts they are facing. In general, we try to allow issues to resolve by using our knowledge to hold the issue in focus. It is our experience that this leads to greater resolution, both in mind and body, and to fuller integration into people's lives.

THE BODY

There are many ways to use the body to help individuals and couples experience, witness, explore, understand, and change their behavior. Often the focus will be on one person of the couple, but we regularly have them do some physical activity together. We will outline below some of the general approaches we use. In most cases we use the body to explore an issue that is already present in therapy. Whether and when we touch or do not touch a specific client is discussed in Appendix 3.

By simply bringing a person's attention to his/her body, particularly to the physical sensations in some part of the body, he/she can: (a) move from talking about something to an experience related to it; (b) move from feelings related to the past to an experience of the present; (c) move from the abstract level, from ideas or metaphors, to the concrete.

To help clients experience or express something more fully or deeply, we can: (a) ask them to perform a movement that we believe will support or amplify their expression or experience; (b) give physical support with a hand on their back. The exact placement of our hand will reflect our assessment of the character position being explored; (c) stimulate a muscle related to the age or issue being explored, in order to help the latent psychological content flow into expression through words, expressive movement, or emotion.

When working with an early character position, where a particular resource may be weak or absent, we might want to help a client have a new experience. By working with the muscles relevant to the issue being worked on, you can help a person to: (a) strengthen his/her boundaries; (b) experience self-support; (c) learn to contain a feeling; (d) learn to ground himself/herself. When the new resource is embodied, it can be particularly empowering for the client to "revisit" the issue that stimulated the work.

When working with a couple it is often useful to have the partner of the person you have been focusing on see and sense the changes in expression, posture, voice, energy, and attitude of the other. One partner can also mirror the other to get a sense of what their experience is. The couple can move further apart and closer together to explore boundary issues. Often a simple holding of hands or a hand used for support will prove very useful. Eye contact, at appropriate times, can also be very powerful.

AN EXAMPLE OF OUR WORK

It will help us to be more specific if we relate some actual work that one of us did. A couple in their early thirties had been married for seven years and had two children. They came in because he had an emotional outburst and could not contain it. She got scared and started getting physical by pushing him. I tried to help them understand the interaction by slowing down the story and going through the interaction step by step. One of the ways I do this is to help people sense what is going on in their bodies as they remember and talk about the incident. As they get in touch with their bodily sensations, they are more able to identify the emotions and impulses that were acted out in the original incident. He had gotten upset because she did not know where some money was. This pushed him back into feeling like he was once again in his disorganized family of origin. There, he had feared everything would col-lapse, and, in the recent interaction, he got very agitated and started yelling and screaming to hide his vulnerability and fear. She had felt shamed by his angry criticism, but that did not consciously register. The next thing she knew she was pushing him. As we talked abut it, she got in touch with her shame. In our discussion, we decided we needed to work to help him contain his acting out impulses and to slow things down so he could become aware of what was underneath. She wanted help to set clearer boundaries and limits as to how much she would allow this behavior to be directed at her. She also needed support to counter her tendency to feel bad when something like this happened and to assume it was her fault.

Looking at this from a characterological perspective, we would be sus-pecting that she is acting from the Will structure, and from the early position of that structure. We call this the "self-sacrificing" position. Her feelings of shame and her assuming guilt are some of the indications here. We could also make this assessment visually from the structure and posture of her body. The origins of this structure in her life will become clearer later. His case is interesting because he is moving between two structures that are in conflict with each other. Normally, he is also in the Will structure, but in the late position. We call this the "judging" position. In this position a person wants to contain all of his feelings. But under stress, he jumps to the late Existence (Emotional) position. This position is characterized by lots of emotional expression, hence the conflict. He uses the late Will as a defense against even sensing the Emotional underneath, and this makes it very difficult for him to accept himself.

Here are some examples of how this material came to be worked on in later sessions. After another occasion at home where she broke out in a sweat when he wanted her to take care of something and she did not know how to manage it, we agreed to look at her tendency to collapse into shame and anxiety. She was the oldest of several children, and her mom had died when she was not yet five. She had felt the responsibility to take care of the family and keep it together at that time, and felt overwhelmed by the responsibility. As we were talking about it, she started to feel overwhelmed. As she was starting to collapse in her spine, I thought it appropriate to give her physical support (see Appendix 3). I sat on the floor about a foot behind her and asked her to lean back until she was just off balance, and then to catch herself, paying attention to how this felt in her body. I had her do this a few times, and then asked her if it would be okay for me to catch her and help her next time. She agreed, and I caught her with both hands against the latissimus dorsi muscles (these are the broad muscles that wrap the back from below the shoulder blades to the waist, and act to pull the upper arm back). I supported her in that place and then slowly pushed her back to a relaxed sitting position. I chose this particular muscle to support because its psychomotor function is self-support in the developmental stage she was acting from, and it also corresponded to the age when she lost her mother.

At first it was hard for her to allow my help and support. She became concerned that her weight would be too much for me or that she would feel weak if she allowed herself to do this. We talked about these responses, and, after a few times, she could let me catch her, support her, and bring her back to a balanced position. Then she started to feel a change in her body. She started to relax and both sensed in her body and realized how much effort she puts into her holding herself together. I kept my hands on her latissimus and we talked about how support feels to her.

She then started to talk more about her mom's death, and I asked her to remember that time and how it felt in the house, how she felt with the relatives who were there, and how her siblings looked. Then I asked her to put herself in the picture and notice how small she was. Throughout this time, I was giving firm support to the latissimus muscles, at the pressure she said felt good. I started to talk to her as someone should have talked to her then, saying "Someone should have explained to you that you were just a little girl, and that your Mom had just died. And you needed support to be sad and grieve and to mourn the loss of your mom. You needed to be taken care of." At this point, her shoulders started to relax, and she started to feel a lot of sensation in her legs and feet. (We relate this to being more embodied and more grounded.) She stayed with that, and I continued to talk to her as if she were that four-year-old, to speak to her from that developmental stage when this had occurred. She said, "It seems as if a cloud is lifting from my head," and started to cry. As the sensation in her head continued to change, we sat there a bit more with the support to the latissimus. Then, when that felt complete, I asked her to sit again on the couch. I showed her how to put a bit of tension in the latissimus as a way of supporting herself and, for the moment, also placed a pillow behind her in the latissimus area. I asked her to remember what had occurred the night before when she broke out in a sweat. From a clear place, she looked at her husband and said, "I can be OK even when I don't know something." Her husband said he was very moved by watching this work she had done and felt compassion for the struggle she experiences when he gets critical. What was remarkable to him was how similar they both were in their history, even though their ways of managing stress were different.

In another session, they came in and he was very agitated and unable to relax. He was disturbed by a medical report he had received and was feeling distressed. He had been lashing out at her, was critical of her, and could not contain his own anxiety. We started to talk about what it was like as he was growing up. In his family there was a lot of neglect, a lack of boundaries. Two of the kids in his family were actually abused or molested by family friends. While talking about this, he became very agitated. There was much tension in his jaw, his talking sped up, and his shoulders and neck tensed. While talking about the lack of sexual boundaries in his childhood, he made a very spontaneous but quick motion with his arms, as if in a fight. I asked him to slow that down and pay attention to the movement, to follow it where it might want to go. The movement developed to a full extension of his arms, as if he were pushing something away. He started to feel his own body more, all the way down to his pelvis. He remembered a memory he had of being a child and lying in bed, wondering if the family friend would come into the room. I suggested that as a child he could not protect his own body and was not able to push away the unwanted advances of the abuser. His response to stress then was to get very agitated and vigilant, or to disassociate. I asked him to stand and do the spontaneous movement again. Standing helped him to feel the support of the ground through his legs and feet. I gave a little resistance with my hands, so he had something to push against. He could sense his own power and stay present. We then talked about how he could not push away as a child and instead got overwhelmed with agitation and stopped feeling his body.

I had the couple both stand and asked her to give him a little resistance and do a slow push hands movement with each other. She was able to really see how useful this movement was in helping him slow down, get into his body, and be more organized and coherent in himself. I suggested they try this out at home whenever he was feeling overwhelmed, and he was eager to do that. At the end of the session, he was able to go through the medical information and start to talk about it without being overwhelmed. They felt closer to each other, first because the partner's vulnerability was available, and also because they again saw how similar they both were.

CONCLUSION

In our work with couples, we try to help people to see their partner's defensive system (character patterns) as a *defensive* system. That they are using it to defend themselves against their own fears and feelings and not to hurt the partner. This can most easily be grasped when one partner sees the other partner being vulnerable. The safety and containment of the therapy room make this more possible. When people have experienced each other's vulnerability, they become more willing to make agreements with each other to help each come out of their defensive postures. Of course, working out exactly how to do this is best done when they are not in the midst of it. By bringing the body into the therapy, a kind of intimacy is reestablished between the twosome. The use of non-verbal techniques is a way to introduce movement into stuck patterns, and many of the skills learned in therapy can be done together outside. As the couple are able to accept their differences in handling feelings and situations, they also become more self-accepting, and this will lead them to be less stuck in their problems and patterns.

REFERENCES

Bernhardt, Peter, and Isaacs, Joel (2000). The Bodymap: A precise diagnostic tool for psychotherapy. *Bioenergetic Analysis* 11(1), 111-140.

Bernhardt, Peter, Bentzen, Marianne, and Isaacs, Joel (1995, 1996). Waking the body ego, part 1 and part 2. *Energy and Character* 26(1), 27(1), 27(2).

Lake, Frank (1966). *Clinical theology*. London. (no longer in print).

Lake, Frank (late 1970s). *Studies in constricted confusion* (Exploration of a Pre-and Perinatal Paradigm). The Clinical Theology Association, Nottingham, England.

Lowen, Alexander (1958). *The language of the body*. Collier Books, and (1975) *Bioenergetics*, Penguin Books.

Macnaughton, Ian (1997). The narrative of the body-mind. *Embodying the mind and minding the body*, 22-34. Ed. I. Macnaughton, Integral Press, N. Vancouver, BC. (A number of the recent articles cited here are contained in this edited collection.)

Marcher, Lisbeth (1992). See, for example: Bernhardt, P. Individuation, mutual connection, and the body's resources. *Pre- and Peri-Natal Psychology Journal* 6(4), 281-293.

Reich, Wilhelm (1949). *Character analysis*. See 3rd Edition, Orgone Institute Press, NY.

APPENDIX 1. The Bodynamic Character Structures

FREUD	ERIKSON	LOWEN	AGE	STRUCTURAL Issues	HYPO-RESPONSE Predominant / EARLY Position	HYPER-RESPONSE Predominant / LATE Position	BALANCED RESPONSE Predominant / HEALTHY Position	Cross Structural Issues
Genital	Puberty		Teen-Age	Research on this structure is not completed. However, the structural issues seem to be integration of adult sexuality and social function. At the same time, the child recapitulates earlier stages of development.				Cognitive Integration
Phallic	Infantile-Genital Locomotor	Four variations of rigidity	7-12 yrs	Solidarity/Performance	Levelling	Competitive	Balancing self and group	
			5-8 yrs	Opinions	Sullen	Opinionated	Opinion-embodying	Sex-Role Identification
			3-6 yrs	Love/Sexuality	Romantic	Seductive	Balancing heart and sexuality	
Anal	Anal-Urethral Muscular	Masochistic	2-4 yrs	Will	Self Sacrificing	Judging	Assertive	
		Psychopathic	8 mo –2.5 yrs	Autonomy	Non-verbal activity changing	Verbal activity changing	Emotionally autonomous	Boundary Formation
Oral	Oral-Respiratory Sensory-Kinesthetic	Oral	1 mo –1.5 yrs	Need	Despairing	Distrustful	Self-satisfying	
		Schizoid	2nd trimester –3 mo	Existence	Mental	Emotional	Secure Being	

APPENDIX 2. The Ten Ego Functions

1. CONNECTEDNESS: Taking in; bonding; opening the heart; accepting support, feeling "backed up"; bonding; heart contact/opening.

2. STANCE IN LIFE: Existential position; stance toward life; poise for action, personal stance; standing on one's own; position on values and norms; orienting (keeping or losing one's head).

3. CENTERING: Filling out (from the inside); being oneself in one's different roles; feelings of self-worth.

4. BOUNDARIES: Boundaries of personal space (energetic boundaries); self assertion (making space for oneself in social contact).

5. GROUNDING AND REALITY TESTING: Ability to stand one's ground, feel rooted and supported by it; relationship to reality; relationship to spirituality.

6. SOCIAL BALANCES: Balancing one's own needs/feelings/desires against others' expectations; balance of pulling oneself together/letting go; balance of facade versus openness in interactions; balancing being oneself with being a group member; balance of managing stress and resolving it.

7. COGNITIVE SKILLS: Orienting cognitive grasp; understanding (getting something well enough to stand forth with it); grasp of reality; ability to apply cognitive understanding to different situations; planning; contemplation/consideration.

8. ENERGY MANAGEMENT: Building charge, containment, and discharge; emotional management; stress management; self-containment; perception and mastery of one's own sensuality.

9. SELF-EXPRESSION: Assertion; asserting oneself in one's roles; forward impetus and sense of direction.

10. INTERPERSONAL SKILLS: Patterns of closeness and distancing; reaching out, gripping, and holding on; drawing towards oneself and holding close; receiving and giving from one's core; pushing away (saying no) and holding at a distance; releasing, letting go.

APPENDIX 3. On Touch

The subject of touch in therapy remains controversial. On the one side, we know that deprivation of touch in infancy can lead to severe personality disorders. On the other side, we fear that the client could be unduly provoked or even exploited by the therapist. Without trying to go deeply into this area (e.g., Macnaughton, 1997), we can say that all of the instances where we use touch are carefully considered. First, we always use a "bounded" touch, so that our own energy is contained. We do not try to do any healing. We are usually either giving support to a muscle or having a person become aware of that muscle. Second, we are careful whom we touch and will generally not do so with people having character disorders, e.g., borderlines and narcissists. Then, we ask permission before touching, say how and where we intend to touch, and give the person the instruction to ask us to stop anytime they are not comfortable with the touch or are even unsure they are comfortable. We do not touch if we have any concerns about how an individual might experience it, or if we have any concerns in ourselves, whether clear or unclear.

If we decide that it is not appropriate to use touch with a particular client, there are still several ways to bring the body into the psychotherapy. A first way would be to have a person focus on body awareness and sensation. The second possibility would be to teach the person how to use the specific muscles related to the issue they were working on. If we suspect the muscles are underelastic, corresponding to missing resources, we will have the person tense them. If we think the muscles are overelastic, corresponding to a rigid or held back ability, we will ask the person to stretch them. These respective actions help the historical attitudes and experiences of the issue being worked on to flow into awareness. A third possibility, and this would be subject to our assessment of the couple, and to their negotiating an agreement each time, would be to have the partner provide the touch. In this latter case, we would then teach the partner exactly how to give the touch.

Working Experientially and Somatically with Couples

Robert M. Fisher

SUMMARY. Working experientially and somatically with couples is a powerful method of accessing, exploring, and transforming both intrapsychic issues and interactional patterns. In this article, a number of methods of working experientially will be described, along with their underlying rationale. Basic assumptions about the nature of couple's difficulties and the role of the therapist also will be explored along with an integrated approach to assessment that provides a solid basis for these dramatic interventions. *[Article copies available for a fee from The Haworth Document Delivery Service: 1-800-342-9678. E-mail address: <getinfo@haworthpressinc.com> Website: <http://www.HaworthPress.com> © 2001 by The Haworth Press, Inc. All rights reserved.]*

KEYWORDS. Experiential, supporting defenses, assessment, assumptions, mindfulness, posture, gestures, movement, somatic signals, physicalizing the interaction, verbal experiments, transference, transformation, integration

Robert M. Fisher, MFT, is a psychotherapist and consultant in private practice in Mill Valley, CA. He teaches marriage and family therapy at John F. Kennedy University and the theories and techniques of body oriented psychotherapy at the California Institute of Integral Studies in San Francisco. He also teaches couples therapy at the post graduate level in many agencies around the San Francisco area. He has just completed a book for Zeig/Tucker on working experientially with couples. He has been a presenter at numerous conferences, including a master presenter at the annual C.A.M.F.T. conference and, most recently, at the USABP conference. He is the publisher of the *Couples Psychotherapy Newsletter* and Director of the Mount Tamalpais Center for Psychotherapy.

Address correspondence to: Robert M. Fisher, 621 Eucalyptus Way, Mill Valley, CA 94941.

[Haworth co-indexing entry note]: "Working Experientially and Somatically with Couples." Fisher, Robert M. Co-published simultaneously in *Journal of Couples Therapy* (The Haworth Press, Inc.) Vol. 10, No. 2, 2001 pp. 91-106; and: *Couples and Body Therapy* (ed: Barbara Jo Brothers) The Haworth Press, Inc., 2001, pp 91-106. Single or multiple copies of this article are available for a fee from The Haworth Document Delivery Service [1-800-342-9678, 9:00 a.m. - 5:00 p.m. (EST). E-mail address: getinfo@haworthpressinc.com].

Jane began the session complaining that she could not rely on Mike. She held herself stiffly, her neck extended above her shoulders like a small girl being a good little soldier. Mike sat nearby looking helpless. She said, "I just can't lean on him." I said, "Let's find out. Let's see what happens if you have an opportunity to actually lean on him. You want to try?" She indicated that she would be interested in this, so I said, "Okay, let's actually have you physically lean against him, and let's find out what comes up inside of you–feelings, thoughts, sensations in your body, beliefs, memories, images, tensions or relaxation, or nothing at all. Why don't you take a moment inside so that you can notice any subtle changes that occur when you let yourself lean on him. And Mike, you can notice what it is like to be leaned on."

After a bit of negotiating, she found a way to do this. She let her head slowly come to rest on his shoulder. After a minute, she looked at me and said, "I can't stand this!" I asked her what was so uncomfortable about it. She told me that it brought up memories of her past boyfriends and her tendency to give herself up in relationships. She said that she had sworn never to let herself do that again. Even though she wanted to lean on him, that was the last thing in the world she would permit herself to do.

I asked her if I could help protect her from losing herself in the relationship. I offered to support the part of her that advised her not to depend on any man. I could also see her body pulling away from him even as she leaned on him, so I also offered to assist her in not leaning. I sat next to her on the couch gently pulling her arm so that she could not manage to lean against him fully. I also whispered in her ear her own words, "Never depend on a man again." As I did this, I could feel her very gradually begin to lean more towards him. My support for her defense allowed her to feel the impulse underneath it. As we continued with this experiment, she experienced more and more of her desire to be taken care of and more ability to actually let in available nourishment from her partner. It became less and less necessary to hold her away from her partner. At this point, I wanted to check in with Mike to see what it was like for him to be in the uncharacteristic role of supporter. He grinned and said that he finally felt useful to her.

A number of experiential interventions were used in this session. These include the use of mindfulness, physicalizing a psychological dynamic, and supporting defenses both verbally and physically. They will be discussed later in this article in greater detail.

THE RATIONALE FOR EXPERIENTIAL PSYCHOTHERAPY

There is a big difference between watching *National Geographic* on television and going to Africa to watch the giraffes come to the watering hole at dusk. There's a difference between discussing chocolate cake and eating it, between thinking about sex and having it. By working with live experience, one performs psychotherapy in vivo as opposed to in vitro. People develop psychological difficulties not just as the result of polite conversation but because of the impact of real experiences. Therefore, it is very important to access real experiences in psychotherapy as opposed to simply talking about them. Psychotherapy comes to life when working experientially. When working this way, both therapist and client no longer need to guess about motivations or possible interpretations for behavior. Instead, they are engaged in developing the client's ability to be connected with him or herself in such a way that this kind of information becomes available in a direct fashion. Rather than discussing change, clients can take actual risks with trying out new behaviors and beliefs immediately in the session.

UNDERLYING ASSUMPTIONS

There are a number of assumptions that underlie this approach to experiential psychology. These are useful to understand and consider, even if you do not agree with them.

The Problem. What, in general, are the causes of the difficulties that couples experience? This question, of course, can be answered in many different ways depending on your theoretical orientation. One possible answer to consider is the following: Each individual in a couple learns early in childhood to adopt certain character strategies in order to cope with difficult situations and people. The strategies were intelligent and creative adaptations to situations that were often hurtful in many profound ways. Over time, however, the very method that once protected the spirit becomes its prison. It becomes limiting and depriving. For instance, if you grew up in a household where no one was paying attention to you, you may have learned that the only way to be noticed was to become intense, active, colorful, and have big problems that are difficult to ignore. This strategy, in fact, may have worked in your family to garner at least a modicum of attention. In an adult relationship, however, this same strategy might overwhelm an intimate partner, leading him or her to turn attention away from you. This, of course, reinforces the underlying belief that no one is interested in really listening to you. Unfortunately, according to the wisdom of the strategy, being ignored is the cue to intensify your expression, thereby unwittingly further alienating your partner.

Bear in mind, however, that people are, in fact, no more their character strategies than they are the cars that they drive. No one is a 1936 Histrionic 230 SX, or a 1952 Borderline convertible with split leather seats. If you fail to recognize this, your relationship with your clients will be limited by your misunderstanding. Your pathologizing of them will substantially affect the intersubjective field between you, and their level of trust and self-disclosure can be impacted.

Unfortunately, the character strategies that we learned as children usually become overgeneralized. What we learned in our family of five becomes generalized to the rest of the world. What was once adaptive becomes limiting and calcified. For instance, Jane learned to be self-reliant and not to depend on anyone when she was still very little because no one in her family attended very closely to her needs. This continued to play itself out in her later relationships with men. She would portray herself as self-reliant and not needing anything. The intimates in her life would consequently treat her accordingly. This, in turn, would prove her core belief that no one was really interested in helping her. Neurosis is maintained with a little help from our friends.

Character strategies are maintained in the present through the interaction with our intimate partners in circular, self-reinforcing dynamics involving both people. The symptoms which distressed couples present in psychotherapy are often a precipitate of these circular patterns.

People are holographic. Their character strategies are revealed in their tone of voice, their pace, their gestures, their posture, their style of doing any small act. Therefore, it is possible to see the evidence of character, core beliefs, and childhood wounds in something as small as the inflection of a woman's voice, or the way in which a man looks at his partner.

People want to change desperately, while at the same time wholeheartedly resisting change. We long for freedom from the self-imposed limitations of our character, yet our defenses usually inform us that they are our allies, and we would be fools to come out from behind their protective cover.

The Role of the Therapist. Every theoretical orientation prescribes a particular role for the therapist. In the approach discussed in this article, the role of the therapist is to assist each person to more fully embody his or her unique self while being in contact with others. This is different from the role of the therapist as an authority, or as an interpreter of their clients' psyches. The therapist becomes the midwife for the gentle unfolding of the self, and becomes an expert in leading clients deeply into their own experience as opposed to being an expert on the content of their psyches.

ASSESSMENT PROCEDURE

In order to intervene effectively, one must be able to assess accurately what is going on with a couple. Every theoretical orientation also has its own approach to assessment. From an Object Relations point of view, for instance, one might look for transference, projection, projective identification, and the interaction of characterological defenses. From a Family Systems point of view, one might look for self-reinforcing, circular relational dynamics. From a Narrative point of view, one might look for the problem saturated stories and the unique outcomes. From a Strategic point of view, one might look for how the ways in which a couple tries to solve their problems actually maintain and exacerbate them. From a Bowen point of view, one might notice where this couple is on the continuum from fusion to differentiation. From a Cognitive Behavioral point of view, one might notice how each person's cognitive distortions and interpretations of the other's behavior lead to distress. Each system examines a couple through different lenses. As far as I can tell, despite claims to the contrary, no system has an exclusive relationship with the truth. It seems useful to be able to assess a couple from a variety of angles and not try to fit a couple into the limitations of one particular lens.

As a way of integrating these many divergent points of view, I believe that it is important to assess a couple by noticing *both* the systemic as well as intrapsychic elements that keep the difficulties in place. For instance, if Laurel is angry with Henry because he is so withdrawn, one might notice a circular quality to their interaction. The angrier she becomes, the more he responds with withdrawal. The more he withdraws, the angrier she becomes. Their interaction is self-reinforcing. It is *also* extremely important to examine the intrapsychic elements that underlie each partner's position in this dance. Where is it that Henry learned about withdrawal? What is familiar about it? How does it protect his heart? What in Laurel is triggered when she notices his unavailability? Has this happened before? Do the wounds from the past intensify how she perceives and feels about Henry when he withdraws? Each person comes to relationship with a history that is replayed in the present in circular self-reinforcing ways. Diagnosis and assessment are most useful when they take into account both of these elements. Accurate assessment of the couple's dynamics leads to appropriate and effective interventions.

EXPERIENTIAL TECHNIQUES

There are many experiential techniques that one can apply to assist a couple in deeply accessing, exploring, and transforming their internal and intrapsychic dynamics. Working with experience brings therapy to life and presents the opportunity to work deeply with the place inside of people where their psyches are still malleable. Below, I will try to expand on the standard repertoire of experiential techniques by including a number of categories of working with experience such as: (1) the use of mindfulness, (2) experiments with posture, (3) experiments with gestures and movement, (4) using somatic signals, (5) physicalizing the interaction, (6) sculptures and metaphors, (7) verbal experiments, (8) supporting defenses, (9) breaking the trance of transference,

(10) transformation, and (11) integration. I will briefly describe each of these and provide short vignettes of how they are applied. Please note that this list is not exhaustive. If a therapist is well grounded in assessment procedures, then working experientially is limited only by their own creativity and imagination. Being able to conceptualize what is transpiring in a couple's dynamics leads directly to appropriate interventions. One can borrow from a variety of other orientations, such as psychodrama, art therapy, movement therapy, and other adjunctive methods, to generate possibilities for working with live experience.

The approach I am proposing is derived primarily from an experiential psychotherapy called the Hakomi Method of Experiential Psychology (Kurtz, 1992). This method was developed by Ron Kurtz as an individual psychotherapy and has been applied to couples therapy by myself and others. In addition to its deep dedication to working with live experience, two of its most distinguishing features are the use of mindfulness and the belief that supporting defenses is more effective than opposing them. This method is also very aware of power imbalance between therapist and client and the potential for harm and violence that can subtly, or not so subtly, be inflicted on clients.

Experiential and somatic approaches to psychotherapy have a long history, starting with Freud's use of transference (an intense experiential event occurring in the session). Virginia Satir worked with family sculptures and stressed the nonverbal aspects of communication. In *Peoplemaking* (Satir, 1972) she writes, "Whenever you say words, your face, voice, body, breathing are talking too" (p. 60). Minuchin asked clients to reenact scenes from their lives outside of therapy. Fritz Perls worked only with people's immediate awareness. Keith and Whitaker wrote, "We presume it is experience, not education that changes families" (Keith and Whitaker, 1982). Napier and Whitaker (1978) wrote, "This approach assumes that insight is not enough. The client must have emotionally meaningful experience in therapy, one that touches the deepest levels of his person" (p. 283). Milton Ericksen and others have also continued to expand upon this tradition. Alexander Lowen (Lowen, 1958) believed that the body was an expression of character:

> The character of the individual as it is manifested in his typical patterns of behavior is also portrayed on the somatic level by the form and movement of the body. The sum total of the muscular tensions seen as a gestalt, that is, as a unity, the manner of moving and acting constitutes the "Body Expression" of the organism. The body expression, the somatic view of the typical emotional expression, is seen on the psychic level as "Character." (p. 15)

The new crop of body psychotherapies such as Integrated Body Psychotherapy, Bodynamics, Core Energetics, Formative Psychology and others are all making their contributions as well.

Any of the techniques from these orientations applied to couples psycho-therapy may be useful, provided that they are based on careful assessment and are not simply accessing experience to create drama. Dramatic therapy is not always good therapy. These techniques can also be particularly effective if they make use of the principles and the techniques of mindfulness.

The Use of Mindfulness. There are many different states of consciousness. When we talk to friends, when we drive our cars, when we teach, when we read, we are generally in the state that might be called ordinary conscious-ness. There is another state of consciousness, which the Buddhists call mind-fulness. Mindfulness is a state of self-observation without judgment or pref-erence. One of the challenges that couples therapists often encounter is how to instill a sense of observing ego into a couple's interaction so that they begin to "act in" this opposed to "acting out." How does one recruit a couple into developing an observing ego through which they can become curious about their behavior and motivations as opposed to blaming their partner for their distress? If this can be accomplished, couples therapy be-comes easy and rewarding. In the absence of this, the therapist becomes a judge or a policeman and is reduced to calming down volatile conversations and providing superficial solutions to deeper problems. Mindfulness is par-ticularly effective in addressing this problem. Here is how it is used:

Prior to introducing any experiential intervention, I ask the couple or the individual involved to become mindful. For instance, I might say, "Take a moment to go inside, to turn your attention inward, so that you can notice any thoughts, feelings, sensations, changes in your breathing, tension or relax-ation, memories or images that might spontaneously arise." I slow my voice down, and sometimes close my eyes in order to model turning my attention inside. This provides a frame in which we can all become curious and non-judgmental about the inner workings of the couple or individual. Once mind-ful, we can then, on purpose, evoke a variety of experiences that can be collaboratively explored.

For instance, I might notice that it is difficult for a wife to listen to her husband complain about her. I might ask them to repeat a small portion of this interaction in mindfulness so that they can notice the subtleties of (1) what occurs inside of her when she hears his complaint, and (2) he can notice the place inside him from which the complaint originates. In one couple that I saw, this was just the case. He would complain, and she would either defend herself or cross-complain. In order to explore this further, I asked him to repeat only one sentence of his complaint. One sentence is a sufficiently small dose so that the partner does not become so overwhelmed that he or she loses his or her observing ego. I asked her to receive this sentence in a state of mindfulness. She didn't have to justify herself, agree or disagree with any-thing. She could simply study her own automatic reaction to his complaint. In essence, they conducted their interaction in slow motion. Instead of defending herself, she noticed how intolerable it was for her to disappoint him. As she stayed with this feeling, she remembered how her parents had never punished her. They just said, "We are so disappointed in you." It was very unlikely that she would have recognized these underlying feelings unless she was in the state of mindfulness. More information becomes available to the conscious mind when mindfulness is utilized.

Any interaction in which the couple engages can be studied in a state of mindfulness in order to bring unconscious material into awareness. If one sets up evocative experiments without mindfulness, the amount of unconscious material that becomes available is limited.

The therapist also needs to be in a state of mindfulness. He or she needs to pay attention not only to the ever-changing internal experiences within him or herself, but more importantly to the moment-to-moment internal experiences of each member of the couple. Tracking internal experience is a major key to working experientially. In addition to tracking the content and themes of session, it is extremely important that the therapist notice non-verbal communications, such as changes in posture, gestures, energy level, breathing, coloration; the presence of beliefs, feelings, pace, volume; the style of walking, sitting, or talking, to name just a few possibilities. Tracking these elements allows the therapist to join with the client and encourage whatever unfolding is trying to take place from his or her psyche. If, for instance, a tear rolls down the cheek of one partner, the therapist might say simply, "Sad, huh?" This simple intervention promotes contact and connection between therapist and client. If a man looks agitated while he listens to his wife complain about him, the therapist might say, "It's hard to hear this, huh?" Carl Rogers taught us to reflect back the meaning of what people say. This kind of empathic mirroring is an essential therapeutic technique. Contact statements go one step further and reflect back people's immediate internal experience. This is very intimate, and lets clients know that the therapist is present with them in a deep way.

Once mindfulness is present, the therapist can design opportunities for the couple and the individuals within it to explore how they are organized psychologically around each other. It is important to take into account each person's characterological contribution to the process as well as the self-reinforcing, circular nature of the interaction in designing these opportunities for study.

Experiments with Posture. How each individual's body is organized around their intimate partner has a substantial impact on their interactions. Here is an example: It took me several sessions to notice that when Sam spoke to Jennifer he had his head tilted slightly upwards. I asked the couple if it would be okay for them to try a little experiment. It is important to ask permission and to let the couple know what you have in mind in advance. I wondered out loud what would happen if he allowed his chin to tilt down just a couple of inches. I asked each person to become mindful of what takes place inside when he made this minor change in his posture. They might notice feelings, sensations, images, memories, changes in muscle tension or in breathing, anything at all that comes up automatically when he performs this slight change. As soon as he let his chin drop, she let out a big sigh. I contacted her experience by saying, "Relieved huh?" She said, "I finally feel like I have a partner!" When I turned to him, I could see that he was less enthusiastic about this change. He said that he felt ambivalent. On the one hand, he liked being down here on the planet, while on the other it felt very scary to him. This provided us with the opportunity to study his beliefs around safety, as well as his methods for protecting himself, which often backfired in his relationship.

Experiments with Gestures and Movement. Gestures and movement often provide a hologram, not only of the individual character strategies of each person, but into the interactional patterns of the couple as well. For example, as I watched Sam and Kathy, I could see that the way they held and moved their ankles was remarkably different from each other. She held her foot tensely upwards and in constant motion, while his foot dangled loosely at the end of his leg. This configuration of ankle tension was a microcosm of their characterological organizations around time and agreements. While she held agreements rigidly and strictly, and believed very much in being on time, he held them casually and loosely, often arriving an hour late for dinner. Simply by discussing the differences in their ankles the couple felt relieved to acknowledge their unique styles. She came in to the subsequent session and said that there was much less conflict between them because she had stopped trying to make him like her. Alternate experiments might have included her trying to make his ankle as tense and poised for action as hers, or, vice versa, him trying to make her ankle as relaxed as his. Conversely, he could have helped her by supporting the tension in her ankle so that she did not have to do it all by herself. Clearly this couple had fallen into the roles of over-functioning and under-functioning. The roles were embodied in the microcosm of their ankles and could be studied and modified somatically.

Using Somatic Signals. The body provides a wealth of information directly from the psyche. The body does not lie as easily as people do with their words. A simple experiment that can reveal how people are organized around intimacy is to ask a couple in mindfulness to move their bodies closer or further apart from each other. As they do this, they can periodically stop to study what is happening inside their bodies. Because they are performing this slowly and in mindfulness, they will begin to notice some of the psychological issues that begin to surface with closeness and with distance. In the rush of their daily lives they would be unlikely to notice the subtle proprioceptive signals that occur as the distance between them changes. For instance, some-one with injuries of inundation in his childhood might begin to experience them in response to his partner moving closer. Someone with injuries of abandonment might begin to experience an awful pit of emptiness as her partner moves further away. In the course of a normal couple's interaction, these subtle signals would remain unnoticed and unconscious. If this experi-ment is performed slowly and in mindfulness, however, these unconscious experiences will begin to emerge into consciousness without the need for interpretation. The clients will simply become more aware of themselves.

A similar experiment is to ask a couple to draw or mark a boundary around each person to symbolize their experience of their personal space. Once drawn, the partner can move into or away from the other's personal space and notice the effect. This helps to elucidate each person's organization around his or her personal boundaries. From here, the couple can explore each person's history around their boundaries and later negotiate how they would like to organize themselves around their own and their partner's boundaries.

Physicalizing the Interaction. Particularly for volatile couples who be-come easily lost in their words and begin to lose any sense of observing ego, it is sometimes useful to develop a physical metaphor for their psychological interaction. Virginia Satir helped families to study their roles and interactions by using family sculptures. In order to symbolize a placator/blamer relation-ship, she might tell one person to stand with a finger pointed down at another person on her knees, pleading and looking up at the other. I prefer to have the couple come up with a physical metaphor on their own. When couples are in a particularly entrenched dynamic, I might ask them to take a moment to close their eyes and imagine walking in a park. As they round a large hedge they see a new sculpture garden with a sculpture of them in this particular difficult interaction. The sculptor has captured the mood, feelings, and each of their postures exquisitely. After the sculpture becomes clear to each of them, they can open their eyes and describe what they have seen. We then select one sculpture for further exploration. This can be accomplished simply by having the couple physically enact the sculpture in mindfulness and inter-nally study the feelings, beliefs, memories, and images that accompany this physical representation of their psyche. Additional insights and information can often be obtained by exaggerating or inhibiting any individual element of the sculpture. For instance, in the sculpture of a pursuer/distancer relation-ship, one person may be standing with her arms outstretched towards the other who is looking away. The relational dynamic as well as its individual history and psychology could be further brought into awareness by asking the woman, in this case, to stretch her hands out even more towards her partner, or by asking the man to turn away even further. Conversely, they could experiment to see what might come up if she dropped her hands, or if he turned his head more towards her. These powerful experiments can evoke deep feelings, core beliefs and graphically demonstrate how the emotionally laden images from the past influence the couple's present dynamics. Prior to leaving the session, it is always important to ask the couple to recast the sculpture in a fashion that would be more nourishing to them.

When intense feelings arise in couple's therapy, the therapist can become torn about whether to work in a focused fashion with the individual with the feelings or to remain concentrated on the couple's dynamics. I have found it useful to work for short periods with one individual in front of his or her partner. This tends to increase empathy and understanding in the relationship. If, however, the listener is too impatient or narcissistic to listen and witness for a while, this needs to be explored as well. Learning how to listen to one's partner's feelings is an integral component of intimacy. Modeling this skill, and exploring it with the couple in therapy, is useful and demonstrates that feelings are not to be feared, but can be held by therapist and partner alike as deep expressions from the self. Feelings, given an environment that is non-judgmental and safe, will unfold themselves. As long as the client is not falling into the vortex of retraumatization, the expression of feelings provides a vehicle for rapidly deepening a relationship.

A couple can also be instructed to come up with a verbal metaphor for their interaction. A metaphor should have a representation for each person, as well as for the interaction between them. Here is an example from my practice: Sylvia was irritated with Harry for being so emotionally unavailable. The more irritated she became, the more withdrawn he became. When asked to come up with a metaphor for this interaction, she came up with the following: "I'm walking across a windswept plain and I see a small cottage. I go to the door and knock. 'Is anybody home?' I hear a voice on the inside say, 'Go away!' I asked what she does then. She smiled, "Then I try to break down the fucking door!" I asked him what he would do in that situation. He replied that he would barricade the door even further. We then began to develop a new metaphor. In this story she walks across the same windswept plain and sees the cottage. She knocks on the door. She hears a voice say, "Go away!" She responds, "I have come with a truckload of mortar and bricks to help you build the walls of your cottage even stronger." I asked him what he would say then. He said, "I'll be right out!" This became a new reference point for the possibility of a different kind of relationship in which she was not so invested in tearing down his defenses thereby permitting him to come out of his withdrawal more readily.

Verbal Experiments. Mary and Jack came to their first session of psychotherapy. Mary talked without stopping or taking a breath for the first 20 minutes. There was a sense of desperation about her pace. When she finally inhaled, I contacted her experience, "You feel rushed inside, huh?" She looked up at me, surprised in her soliloquy. I said, "How about I tell Jack something he could say to you, and you can notice whatever happens inside when he says this? I promise it won't be mean." She nodded assent. I wrote on a piece of paper, "Mary, I see you and I hear you." I handed it to Jack and asked him to say it when she was ready. As soon as he spoke the words, she started to cry. She looked up at her husband and said, "I have been waiting our whole relationship for you to say that." I said, "I think you have been waiting longer than that."

Everyone enters relationships hoping that their partner will finally provide the specific kind of emotional nurturance that they did not have as a child. We are all very disappointed when this does not occur. If the therapist, with her knowledge of her clients, can come up with a sentence that distills the words of grace that each person would most like to hear, then an experiment can be constructed in which the partner can say those very words. Again, it is important to invoke mindfulness prior to beginning. While a verbal statement is potentially nourishing, the most common result is that the defense to the nourishment is clearly evoked and can be explored in vivo.

Verbal experiments can be constructed to explore any area in the couple's relationship. Either the therapist or intimate partner can deliver a short and simple sentence that is potentially nurturing to the other partner who is in mindfulness. This is different from an affirmation in that the expected result is often disbelief, suspicion, or opposition to the statement. The purpose of this is to provide an opportunity to explore an individual's or a couple's resistance to nourishment. Some other examples might be: "It's OK to be vulnerable," "You can show your anger," "Your sexuality is welcome," "You're safe here," or "You don't have to do anything for me to love you."

Supporting Defenses. Many psychotherapists believe that it is their job to oppose and eliminate their client's defenses. This puts them in direct opposition to their client's most favored allies. Many intimate partners also seem to believe that it is their job to take down their partner's defenses. Rather than pay them for this service, however, their only wages are resentment and an intensification of their partner's defenses and protective maneuvers. The distress that most couples experience is often a direct result of one or both partners trying to eliminate the defensive strategies of the other. Neither in therapy, nor in intimate relationships does this seem to be a particularly effective procedure. In direct contrast to this approach, I would suggest that a more useful method for dealing with defenses is to help support them. People feel very alone in the defensive methods. They have been told more than once that they should not be this way. Consequently, they may feel resistant or guilty about their defenses. None of this serves to reduce the intensity of the defense. If the therapist can create a situation in which one partner can support the other's defenses instead of attempting to eliminate them, a re-markable change can occur. Here is an example, in short form:

"You're killing yourself, Jack," said Sally, "I want you to quit smoking." Jack replied, "It's my life, and I'll do whatever I want to do!" So the discussion began in the session. I turned to Jack and said, "This is a fight for freedom, huh?" He nodded. I asked him to close his eyes for a moment. For the next five minutes, his girlfriend and I assembled around him an army of sand tray figures that would be his soldiers in his fight for freedom. There were lions, Darth Vader, soldiers, fierce demons, Sumo wrestlers, and even a bride. I asked him to open his eyes and told him that this was his army and it also included at least two other people, his girlfriend and me. We, too, would fight for his right to be free. Carefully, he picked up each figure, one at a time, slowly turning it around in his hand and replacing it on the couch. Finally he spoke to his girlfriend, "I've got what I wanted, now what do you need?" She had become his ally.

Supporting defenses can be verbal or it can be physical. For instance, if a client is crying while hiding her face in her hands, I might ask her boyfriend or partner to help her hide her face. This is an example of physically support-ing the defense. The support can even be metaphorical as in the story of the woman who brought a truckload of bricks and mortar to support the walls of her husband's metaphorical cottage against intrusion. It can also be verbal. In one verbal experiment, I started by saying to the couple, "It's OK to be vulnerable to each other." They mindfully tracked what came up inside. He reported that "The committee" said, "Why should you be open to someone who has hurt you like that?" We continued the session with her asking him to open up to her again. I sat next to him and, with his permission, supported the part of him which advised against being open. I told both of them that the purpose of this exercise was to find out more about "the committee." After a while, he turned to me and said, "I don't want to listen to you any more. This is not how I want to live my life." By externalizing the defense, he gained a new perspective on it and how much it limited him. He exercised his right to not defend.

Breaking the Trance of the Transference. We all superimpose emotionally laden images from the past onto our present partners. This is the work of transference. We hope that we have finally found partners who will not repeat the injuries from our past, yet we treat them in ways to ensure that they will act out patterns that are familiar to us. We project the ghosts of our past onto our present intimates in the hopes of resolving or healing past wounds. Unfortunately, our partners often fail to appreciate these acts. In the spirit of riding the horse in the direction that it is running, I often suggest that we let the transference play itself out, rather than resisting it. This means that the recipient of the projection from the past is instructed not to try to fight it or correct any misimpressions, but to allow herself to be a representative of all the people that have inflicted this particular emotional injury on her partner. Her partner then has the opportunity to do or say anything he wants (as long as it is not violent) to this stand-in for all the perpetrators from the past. It is important before ending the session to help the person distinguish between his present-day intimate partner and the person who wounded him in his past.

Here is an example: Joanne was upset at Harry: "I say let's go to movies, but you say no. I say let's have Chinese food, but you say no. I say let's make love, but you say no. I just can't stand it anymore." I was wondering if she was asking in a way that was alienating him, so I suggested that she bring the argument into the present and ask him for something she would like right now. I could then see clearly that when she did ask for something she wanted, she was not particularly demanding or offensive, but that he was triggered. I asked him what it was like hearing her request. He said, "She's just trying to control me." I suggested he take a moment just to stay with that feeling and notice if there is anything familiar about it. Were there other people he felt this way about? I asked him to imagine all the people who tried to control him positioned behind her, and I asked her indulgence to be all those people. Once assembled, it included everyone from Adolph Hitler to the multinational corporations raping the rain forests, from his grandmother to the Bible. They were all symbols of oppression. I told her that the good news was that he was in bed with Adolph Hitler, not her! She did not need to take his rejection personally. We then gave him an opportunity to speak directly to all these people through their representative and to experience the satisfaction of finally completing his communication, "You can't control me!"

Transformation. No discussion of couples therapy would be complete without a note on how transformation of couple's dynamics takes place. As discussed earlier, people limit themselves through the utilization of overgeneralized character strategies. The strategies are maintained and encouraged in their interactions with their intimate partners on an ongoing basis. One of the purposes of couples psychotherapy is to help each individual more fully embody his or her own uniqueness and reduce the limiting effect of these characterological constraints. Couples therapy is also a place to explore how each person is organized around his/her partner and to make conscious the repetitive, circular, and self-reinforcing patterns of interaction so that the couple will have a choice to interact more from their essential selves with each other.

Insight, however, is rarely enough for transformation. Understanding how one limits oneself through the constraints of character strategies and their attendant beliefs and models of the world is an important first step in transformation. Bringing insight into live interaction with one's intimate partner involves taking what is usually perceived as a risk. It is a risk to show oneself in a more vulnerable fashion than one's defenses would habitually allow. This is not for the faint of heart! The job of the therapist is to look for opportunities in which these risks can gently be taken in small increments, and to provide the support necessary for each client to step over this threshold into greater differentiation. In the opening vignette, for instance, Jane can expand her psychological repertoire by experimenting with leaning on Mike. This is a risk. Her character strategy informs her that it would be unsafe to do so, yet her self-reliance is compromising her ability to take in nourishment from the relationship. In the sanctity of the session, she can experiment by taking a risk to let herself be more supported by her partner than she usually permits.

Integration. Once change begins to occur in psychotherapy, it is important to find ways to integrate these changes into the daily habits and routines in which couples engage. It is very useful to anchor change in people's physical bodies, as well as to encourage them to role play new patterns while still in the therapy room. If, at the end of a session a man is feeling more emotionally available to his partner, for instance, the therapist might say, "Let yourself look at her with softer eyes." If a woman, as a result of her work in therapy, is more able to set limits for her partner, the therapist might ask her to first assume the posture of someone who is unable to set limits, and then to assume the posture of her newfound ability. From here, one can explore what each of these is like for her inside, as well as how her partner experiences her in this new structural form.

The termination phase of therapy begins when positive changes begin to stabilize and the destructive patterns that brought a couple into therapy have decreased both in intensity and in frequency. Intimacy is enhanced and can be tolerated by both partners on an ongoing basis. At this point, it is important to review and continue to integrate the changes that have already been made. Integration techniques such as those mentioned above fill the bulk of the session. The couple can role play difficult situations in the session and apply what they have learned in order to further stabilize the new interactional patterns. The therapist and the couple can discuss possible places in which they could have difficulty and review what they have leaned that would be useful in these occurrences. Much of couples therapy can be organized around exploring the deficits in the individual and in the couple's psychology. In the termination phase, it is important also to reinforce their strengths and resources as well as explore further how they can deepen their closeness.

CONCLUSION

In summary, working with immediate experience provides both the therapist and clients with the opportunity to access core material more readily. Prior to engaging in any such interventions, however, because of the power of these techniques, it is important to take time to accurately assess both the intrapsychic and the systemic aspects of the couple's interactions. While there are many possibilities for experiential interventions, using mindfulness is particularly important in accessing deep psychic material. It can be used in conjunction with any other experiential approach. How the therapist positions herself in relationship to the client's defenses can also spell the difference between success and failure in psychotherapy. The recommendation here is to find ways in which both the therapist and the intimate partner can support rather than oppose defenses. Working with experience can generate immediate change in the couple's relationship. The format of couples psychotherapy lends itself to experiential interventions because an important element of each client's life, the intimate partner, is actually in the room with them. Existing intrapsychic and systemic elements can be explored in vivo. Opportunities to try out different interactional styles and new beliefs are omnipresent.

REFERENCES

Keith, D.V., and Whitaker, C.A. (1982). Experiential-symbolic family therapy. In A.M. Horne and M.M. Ohlsen (Eds.), *Family counseling and therapy*. Itasca, IL: Peacock.

Kurtz, R. (1992). *Body centered psychotherapy, the Hakomi method*. Mendocino, CA: Liferhythm Press.

Kurtz, R., and Prestera, H. (1976). *The body reveals*. New York: Harper and Row.

Lowen, A. (1958). *The language of the body*. New York: Collier Books.

Napier, A., and Whitaker, C.A. (1978). *The family crucible*. New York: Harper and Row.

Satir, V. (1972). *Peoplemaking*. Palo Alto, CA: Science and Behavior Books.

Method Acting and Gestalt Therapy with Couples

James Pugh
Bree Patrick Luck
Edward W. L. Smith

SUMMARY. Techniques taken from Method acting may be useful therapeutic tools and may lend themselves to adoption by Gestalt therapists. Similarities between the goals and procedures of Method acting and Gestalt therapy are described in some detail. The importance and effectiveness of enacted fantasy are discussed, and techniques of Method acting are described in terms of their relation to Gestalt theory. The importance and application of these techniques to Gestalt therapy with couples are discussed. *[Article copies available for a fee from The Haworth Document Delivery Service: 1-800-342-9678. E-mail address: <getinfo@ haworthpressinc.com> Website: <http://www.HaworthPress.com> © 2001 by The Haworth Press, Inc. All rights reserved.]*

James Pugh, PhD, is Assistant Professor of Psychology at Georgia Southern University. He has had extensive training in Gestalt and psychomotor psychotherapies and approximately fifteen years of professional work in psychotherapy. In addition to his university work, Dr. Pugh continues to do psychotherapeutic work in a medical setting.

Bree Patrick Luck, BS, is an actor, writer, and director who was recently seen in Clint Eastwood's "Midnight in the Garden of Good and Evil." Ms. Luck received her BS in Psychology from Georgia Southern University and is currently a master's candidate in New York University's Drama Therapy program.

Edward W. L. Smith, PhD, is Professor of Psychology and Coordinator of Clinical Training at Georgia Southern University. He has published six books, most on Gestalt therapy. A Diplomate of the American Board of Professional Psychology (ABPP), he is a long-time member of the editorial board of the *Journal of Couples Therapy.*

[Haworth co-indexing entry note]: "Method Acting and Gestalt Therapy with Couples." Pugh, James, Bree Patrick Luck, and Edward W. L. Smith. Co-published simultaneously in *Journal of Couples Therapy* (The Haworth Press, Inc.) Vol. 10, No. 2, 2001, pp. 107-114; and: *Couples and Body Therapy* (ed: Barbara Jo Brothers) The Haworth Press, Inc., 2001, pp. 107-114. Single or multiple copies of this article are available for a fee from The Haworth Document Delivery Service [1-800-342-9678, 9:00 a.m. - 5:00 p.m. (EST). E-mail address: getinfo@haworthpressinc.com].

KEYWORDS. Method acting, Gestalt therapy, character integrity, communication, awareness, enacted fantasy, concentration, presentification

Through the character of Harry Haller, known as the "Steppenwolf,"
Hermann Hesse (1969, p. 55) demonstrates for us that "every strength may
become a weakness (and under some circumstances must)." If we take
Hesse's insight seriously and relate it to therapeutic procedures, we may well
conclude that any technique, strong as it may be, will at times become a
weakness. That is, the strength of a therapeutic procedure may also be its
weakness.

The appeal of the Gestalt approach, for many, is its technical versatility.
Aside from its philosophical underpinning and its theory of healthy and
unhealthy personality dynamics, the range of its techniques may be highly
appealing. Furthermore, within the philosophical and theoretical framework
of the Gestalt approach, techniques from other approaches are welcome.
Gestalt therapy lends itself well to technical integrations (Smith, 1997). By
means of its inherent versatility with respect to technique, and its comfort
with technical eclecticism, the Gestalt approach may have options at whatever point a particular technique's "strength may become a weakness."

Effective therapy can take place at any of several levels of working. A
model for the levels at which persons in therapy may work has been provided
by the third author (Smith, 1985). The model suggests four levels, with
increasing degrees of potency, accompanied by decreasing levels of safety.
The levels are as follows: (1) Talking About; (2) Fantasy; (3) Enacted Fantasy; (4) Literal Activity. The increase in potency, and decrease in safety from
level to level is a function of increasing "realness" of the experience. With
each successive level, there is a greater immediacy of contact, which accrues
through the following three factors:

1. Increasing bodily (musculoskeletal) involvement (a dimension of abstract [levels 1 and 2] to concrete [levels 3 and 4]);
2. Increasing focus of words and actions on a target person or personifica-
   tion (level 1, words *about* the target; levels 2 and 3, words and actions
   directed at a symbolic target; level 4, words and actions directed at a
   literal target);
3. Increasing emotional (autonomic nervous system) arousal.

At this point, it is probably obvious that all of these levels of work are of
potential value. Taking into consideration the degree of psychological intensity judged appropriate for the person in therapy at a given time, the range of
technical expertise of the therapist, and practical considerations (such as
unavailability of a person for a literal encounter due to death, refusal to
cooperate, or inconvenience), the optimal level of working can be chosen.

One could easily argue that the forte of the Gestalt approach is its work at the level of enacted fantasy. The procedures by which Gestalt work is most often identified, such as the empty chair dialogue, are certainly found at this level. As noted above, Gestalt is open to technical integration, and at the level of enacted fantasy, method acting seems a likely and potentially very powerful candidate.

Before explicating Method acting, however, it would be helpful to explore the techniques found in Gestalt itself. By laying such groundwork, it will be easier to understand the comfortable fit of Method acting in the Gestalt framework.

In organizing and understanding the relationships of techniques in the Gestalt approach, one may well conclude that *all Gestalt techniques are ways of furthering the here-and-now experience, of expanding one's awareness of her or his embodied self in the moment.* The techniques, themselves, in the service of the here-and-now experience, can be seen as promoting either *concentration* or *presentification* (Smith, 1975).

Concentration promoting techniques involve an "opening up to" and "staying with" one's contact with the inner or outer world. By decreasing distractions and focusing on one's experience, that experience becomes more vivid and awareness is enhanced. Slowing down one's pace, repeating a behavior, and exaggerating the intensity of a behavior are all ways of increasing awareness-enhancing concentration.

Presentification, a term introduced into the Gestalt literature by Claudio Naranjo (1970), refers to the bringing of the remembered past or the anticipated future into present experience. It involves a psychodramatic acting out of the memory or fantasy, making it a here-and-now experienced event. This is role-play in its profound sense.

With this background and structure set, let us now explore Method acting.

Method actors, with their various performance styles and techniques, have one common goal–to attain a sense of character integrity throughout the strain and monotony of performance. Any attempt to boil down all of Method acting to a few chosen techniques is as futile as condensing all the procedures of Gestalt therapy to the practices of a single therapist. There are nearly as many "methods" for acting as there are Method actors. However, most of the modern variations of method (or systematic) acting are derived from the techniques established by the Russian dramatic theorist, Constantin Stanislavski, and are perpetuated by the teachings of the late Lee Strasberg. The fundamental philosophy supported by these founders of Method acting is this: In order to move closer to creating a genuine character within a fantasy, the actor must develop his or her ability to relax, concentrate, and find the sense of truth that supports a scene (Hull, 1985).

Lee Strasberg, in his effort to stress the importance of relaxation, claimed that "In order to act, the actor must relax" (Schechner, 1964, pp. 119-120). Deep and holistic relaxation, accomplished by a combination of mental, vocal, and muscular exercises, prepares the actor's instrument for action and allows the performer to charge into a fantasy unencumbered by blocks of emotional or physical tension. This fundamental technique is employed as a priming mechanism before assuming a character role, whether in rehearsal or performance, and regardless of the complexity of the scene. No fantasy is simple. Each involves "real" emotions and "real" actions. Relaxation gives the performer the security to fulfill the emotional and physical needs of the character and opens her or him to a wealth of emotions. According to Strasberg, after relaxation "Emotion that has been habitually held back suddenly gushes forth. The actor becomes real . . . He unveils totally unsuspected aspects of himself . . . with such a degree of ease and authority that he seems literally to have taken off a mask" (Hethman and Strasberg, 1965, pp. 92-93). Relaxation liberates the mind and body from the confines of tension and promotes a truthful enactment of a character within a fantasy.

Concentration, another tenet of Method acting, is "the process of focusing one's mind on an object or objects" (Hull, 1985, p. 33). In order to compel a fantasy, the actor must be able to deal with imaginary elements as though they were genuine. The ability to do this is developed through drills which increase sensitivity to everyday events. In sensory concentration exercises, the actor focuses on a single object, recognizing its heft, shape, color, texture, odor, and sound. The individual then attempts to recreate the object in a verbal description or rendering of the object, and notes any omissions or deviations from the original.

As the actor's technique improves, the concentration exercises progress from physical to more complex emotional levels. One advanced technique, the narrative (or inner) monologue, requires the performer to vocalize the imagined thoughts of a scripted character along with the actual written dialogue. This allows the actor to flesh out the particulars of a role and to articulate the intentions that lie at the root of the character's behavior. While relaxation opens the performer to a vast array of emotions, concentration focuses the actor on the resonant specificities of a scene.

The ability to concentrate allows the performer to approach the third and most distinguishing tenet of Method acting: finding and inhabiting the emotional truth within a scene. Whereas classical conceptions of performance propogate the notion of pretending, that is, of *seeming* to be a character, Method acting insists upon the actor maintaining an immediacy of action and reaction by *being* the character. Performance is based on studied and actual personal events. Through two techniques, sense memory and emotional memory, the actor observes and then "relives" actual physiological reactions to stimuli rather than imagining what he or she would do if an imagined stimulus were present. Thus the reactions are emotional rather than analytical.

In developing sense memory, the individual strives to recreate an event as perceived by all the five senses. This begins with the actor realizing her or his own sensitivity to experience. In the most basic drills, the goal in each exercise is to recreate a moment truthfully by imagining and recreating sensations such as: making a sandwich, feeling the sunlight, or hearing a harsh sound. Sense memory forces the actor to experience each moment as it arrives, and to abandon prescribed manners of responding to a given stimulus.

The use of affective or emotional memory is even more indispensable to the creation of a realistic fantasy, for it synthesizes the use of both sense memory and also the memory of specific emotions to create a cohesive rendering of a situation (Hull, 1985). The actor uses affective memory by recreating the stimuli that caused a certain emotion, parallel to the one needed in a given fantasy or scene. To illustrate, if a character in a scene needs to experience a feeling of abandonment, the actor could recreate a childhood moment in which he or she felt abandoned. Instead of merely remembering the event, the actor recreates sensations surrounding the event–the smells, sights, and sounds of the stimuli that provoked the desired emotion. This prohibits the actor from mimicking events and invites him or her genuinely to experience the emotions. It is important to note that emotional memory exercises do not require the actor to experience the exact circumstances of the scene, rather, the drills encourage the actor to find *emotional parallels* to the character's situation. This is not only safer for the actor, but it also forces the performer to develop a sense of empathy with the character.

Relaxation, concentration, sense memory, and emotional memory are the four primary tools that allow Method actors to create genuine characters within a fantasy. The exercises do require a considerable amount of energy and skill, but their complexity should not deter non-actors from taking advantage of their merits. In fact, it seems that these basic techniques of Method acting could be applicable in a therapeutic environment.

Gestalt therapy and Method acting share some common assumptions and values that encourage the mutual enrichment of each from the other. Quoting from above, the common goal of all forms of Method acting is "to attain a sense of character integrity." Gestalt therapists also attempt to help their clients to attain integration, which entails integrating disowned aspects of the self and being who one truly is. The analogous task of the actor is to "be who the character they are playing really is." Method acting insists that merely to say the correct line and perform the correct actions do not, by themselves, constitute good acting. The actor must be the character, experiencing all the feelings that the character experiences and communicating them to the audience.

In Method acting, that sense of character integrity is attained through relaxation, concentration, and finding the sense of truth. Relaxation is developed through a series of exercises, and, as one's ability to relax improves, one has greater capacity for awareness. In particular, emotional awareness appears to be facilitated by the use of these exercises. In Gestalt, awareness is considered to be an essential element of effective therapy. In the healthy personality, as needs develop, they emerge into awareness, resulting in the mobilization of energy in order to engage the environment for the purpose of meeting the need. As a need is satisfied, it recedes into the background and another need becomes foreground. Without awareness, however, this healthy process becomes impossible: one is unlikely to fulfill successfully those needs of which one is unaware. Over time, many unmet needs may continue to beckon, constituting the unfinished business that often is the "stuff" of so much therapy. Only by enhancing our awareness do we become able to complete these unfinished gestalts and attend, uninterrupted, to our current needs.

Gestalt assumes that bodily tension serves as a means to block emotional awareness and expression. By tensing muscles, we can "freeze" our energy flow and our body awareness, thereby insulating ourselves from unpleasant emotions, such as anger, fear, or hurt. As we relax, we become more aware of our bodies and the emotions that are intimately associated with body sensations. We also allow movement of energy in our bodies, leading to emotional expression and even more heightened awareness. This heightened awareness also leads to the action and engagement that can result in the satisfaction of our needs. In this sense, Gestalt offers a prescription for healthy living as well as therapy for past problems.

Awareness often is blocked if there is a conflict between our true selves and the selves we present to others (the persona). We often prefer to present ourselves as reflecting in truth the ideals we hold; our true self rarely matches the ideal, however, and we often disown those aspects of ourselves that are discordant with who we think we should be. A problem arises if the discrepancy is so great that we refuse to be aware of our true nature. Perls was fond of quoting Nietzsche as saying, "Memory and Pride were fighting. Memory said, 'It was like that,' and Pride said: 'It couldn't have been!' And Memory gave in" (Perls, 1969, p. 2). We remember (and think of ourselves) as we wish to be, not as we are or were. For the client, the task is to experience and communicate his/her true character; for the Method actor, the task is to experience and communicate the truth of the enacted character, so that the actor indeed "seems literally to have taken off a mask," as Strasberg states (Hethman and Strasberg, 1965, p. 93).

For the Method actor, awareness enables the experience and expression of emotions, needs, and wants of the character, resulting in a more realistic portrayal. For the client in Gestalt therapy, awareness enables the experience and expression of emotions, needs, and wants, resulting in the satisfaction of those needs and wants. Because the goals are so similar, exercises from one discipline could have application to the other.

Concentration exercises are used both by Method actors and by Gestalt therapists in order to enhance awareness and intensify experience. Concentration exercises in Gestalt often involve focus on sensory impressions of objects, colors, smells, air movements, etc., as well as focus on body sensations, such as tension, pain, numbness, or energy. One such exercise, called shuttling, may involve deliberately alternating between focus on external and internal stimuli (Perls, Hefferline, and Goodman, 1951). By concentrating on such stimuli, we can intensify the experience and enhance our awareness. When we focus on internal stimuli, we are likely to intensify the emotional experience that often accompanies sensory cues. One very important Gestalt concentration exercise is to exaggerate a sensation, tension, or movement. For example, if we become aware of muscle tension in our shoulders, we focus our attention on that sensation and then exaggerate the muscular tension. Doing so is a very intense form of concentration and often allows us to discover emotions that have been blocked by the muscle tension. Concentration through exaggeration allows into awareness emotions that have been blocked or disowned, thus allowing us to experience and express our character integrity.

It is this character integrity that both the actor and the Gestalt therapist attempt to promote. In the phrase employed earlier, the actor must find the sense of truth that supports the scene. Much of the truth of the scene is derived from the truth of the character, the character integrity. Method acting and Gestalt seek to bring any event, whether remembered, future, or imaginary, into the present. The focus is on the direct *experience* rather than a cognitive analysis. The actor seeks to convince the audience that the events are really taking place, not merely being enacted. The client also seeks to experience the event as if it is occurring in the present. To the degree that both the actor and the client are successful, the event is experienced as if it is really occurring.

In both instances it is through the character integrity that the situation becomes real. The Method actor must "live" the scene and must embody and communicate the truth of the character to the audience. Clients in couples therapy also must live their scenes and must embody and communicate their truth to each other. Each must embody his or her true self and communicate that true self to the partner. That kind of genuineness, truly being oneself, is the only basis for really truthful communication. Like actors, clients must do more than simply *say* the truth; they must *be* the truth. In the couples session, then, enacted fantasy is the same as literal activity, with its greater intensity and impact. Both Method acting and Gestalt therapy seek the character integrity that permits such emotional intensity and truthful communication to occur, and each has much to offer the other.

REFERENCES

Hesse, H. (1969). *Steppenwolf.* New York: Bantam.

Hethman, R. H., and Strasberg, L. (1965). *Strasberg at the actor's studio.* New York: Viking Press.

Hull, L.S. (1985). *Strasberg's method as taught by Lorrie Hull.* Woodbridge, CT: Ox Bow Publishing.

Naranjo, C. (1970). Present-centeredness: Technique, prescription, and ideal. In J. Fagan and I. Shepherd (Eds.), *Gestalt therapy now* (pp. 47-69). Palo Alto, CA: Science and Behavior Books.

Perls, F. (1969). *In and out the garbage pail.* Toronto: Bantam Books, Inc.

Perls, F., Hefferline, R., and Goodman, P. (1951). *Gestalt therapy: Excitement and growth in the human personality.* New York: Dell Publishing Co.

Schechner, R. (1964). Working with live material: An interview with Lee Strasberg. *Tulane Drama Review, 9*(1) 119-120.

Smith, E. (1975). Altered states of consciousness in Gestalt therapy. *Journal of Contemporary Psychotherapy, 7*(1) 35-40.

Smith, E. (1985). *The body in psychotherapy.* Jefferson, NC: McFarland.

Smith, E. (Ed.). (1997). *The growing edge of Gestalt therapy.* Highland, NY: The Gestalt Journal Press.

Index

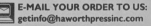
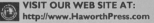